SHOOTING PEOPLE

SHOOTING PEOPLE

Adventures in Reality TV

---◆---

SAM BRENTON and REUBEN COHEN

VERSO

London · New York

First published by Verso 2003
© Sam Brenton and Reuben Cohen 2003
All rights reserved

The moral rights of the authors have been asserted

1 3 5 7 9 10 8 6 4 2

Verso
UK: 6 Meard Street, London W1F 0EG
USA: 180 Varick Street, New York, NY 10014-4606
www.versobooks.com

Verso is the imprint of New Left Books

ISBN 1-85984-540-1

British Library Cataloguing in Publication Data
A catalogue record for this book is available from the British Library

Library of Congress Cataloging-in-Publication Data
A catalog record for this book is available from the Library of Congress

Typeset in Garamond by YHT Ltd
Printed in the USA by R. R. Donnelley & Sons Ltd

For our brothers, Nick and Harry

CONTENTS

1

GAMEWORLDS

Sinisa Savija threw himself under a train in July 1997. A month before his death, he was the first person to be evicted from the island setting of a new game show, *Expedition Robinson*, to be broadcast on Swedish network SVT. His widow told the newspaper *Aftonbladet* that 'He was a glad and stable person when he went away, and when he came back he told me "They are going to cut away the good things I did and make me look like a fool, only to show I was the worst, and that I was the one that had to go." '

SVT almost pulled the show. Critics condemned the series before a single episode was screened, though the producers denied that Savija's death was connected to the programme, claiming he had long-standing psychological problems and was, after all, a Bosnian refugee. Legislators tabled questions about the affair, and the producers received death threats. Savija's presence was diminished in post-production, and the video diary segments in which contestants explained their eviction votes were cut, to prevent the airing of ill words about the dead. Nonetheless, first reviews were brutal, denouncing the show's crudely Darwinian ethos and general tastelessness. Alarmed by the negative coverage, the station suspended *Expedition Robinson* and the commissioning editor resigned. Three weeks later, when an inquiry exonerated the producers of responsibility for Savija's death, the programme returned to the airwaves, and quickly won impressive ratings. By the end of its run *Expedition Robinson* was Sweden's top-rated show, with mass press coverage of contestants, and the winner, Martin Melin, fêted as a celebrity and the nation's most eligible male. The format was clearly potent. Its novel combination of real people and an artificial dramatic setting won a loyal audience and generated great press interest. The international TV markets pricked up their ears. *Survive!*, the format on which the Swedish show was based, has since been sold in some twenty territories. In the summer of 2000 the final episode of the American version of the format, *Survivor*, won an audience of 51,000,000.

The *New York Times* described the show as 'Cinéma vérité with an Orwellian aura', saying that *Survivor* 'breaks the mould of comedies, dramas and news programmes'. As Savija's widow told *Aftonbladet*: 'It's not a game when you choose ordinary people and put them under great pressure, constantly in front of the camera.' The show's desert island setting, forty-day duration and institutionalised war of all-against-all became the whole world for contestants during filming. In the words of Mark Burnett, executive producer of the American series, 'The barriers between TV and Survival, between what's real and what's not real, will be blurred in the total immersion into a quest to outwit, outlast, and outplay one's fellow castaways.'[1] The winners of *Survivor* in the US and UK walked away with a million in local currency. Burnett and CBS would later be sued for alleged game fixing, only to counter-sue the plaintiff, a lawyer and former contestant, for harassment, extortion, and 'a campaign of smears'. This was not the only lawsuit filed in the wake of *Survivor*'s success. The format's creator later initiated litigation against the makers of the next big reality show, and the most globally successful – *Big Brother*, owned by Endemol Netherlands B.V.

The *Big Brother* premise sounds simplistic, and does not in itself communicate any sense of how compulsive its action would prove to be for millions of viewers: a group of extroverts are sequestered in a house covered by remote and hidden cameras, and their daily lives recorded for a period of months. Each week, the housemates nominate two of their number for eviction, with the public deciding the outcome in an open vote. Little happens in the house, and tasks are set to alleviate the tedium, also providing an impetus for teamwork. The last man or woman standing wins a large cash prize.

The impact of *Big Brother* went beyond a ratings triumph, achieving as much for and through new media as it did for television. In a far-sighted reading of changing markets, Endemol established the show as a presence across

---

1. The *New York Times*, quoted in Mark Burnett and Martin Dugard, *Survivor: The Ultimate Game*, TV Books Inc, 2000.

the web, cable channels and mobile phone networks. *Big Brother* houses across Europe were online around the clock, with web cams beaming footage to the desperately addicted, text message updates were available, and a range of national variations enabled viewers to affect the circumstances of life in the house. In the summer of 2000, while *Survivor* was changing the broadcasting landscape in the US, housemate Nick Bateman of *Big Brother UK* was ejected after breaking the rules of the game. The event became a watershed in Britain's online history, with hundreds of thousands of office workers logging on to see the confrontation between Bateman and his fellow housemates. When series two was aired in 2001, an eighteen-hour daily broadcast on cable channel E4 backed up the terrestrial update bulletins and web streams. *Big Brother* was multichannel, multimedia and very nearly live.

The first series generated a long series of front-page headlines in the traditionally news-slow summer, with family, friends and ex-lovers of contestants selling their stories to Britain's red-top tabloids. One week saw twenty-five tabloid front pages dedicated to the show. This was repeated in 2001, with tales of the contestants routinely pushing that summer's other big national popularity contest off the front pages; much to the dismay of politicians and other guardians of national life, *Big Brother* had proven more interesting to readers and authors of the popular press than the general election. On 30 May, a week before polling day, 4.3 million people watched the BBC's ten o'clock news bulletin. At the same time, 4.4 million watched *Big Brother*.

The ratings for *Big Brother UK* were amongst the highest achieved by the screening network, Channel 4, but this made up only part of the picture. During the first series, the official *Big Brother* website was for some weeks the most visited and watched in Europe (with a high degree of 'stickability', or average length of visit, the most crucial factor in catching dwindling revenue from e-advertising). Over the course of the second series, 16,021,671 votes were cast for the eviction of contestants, with over 7,000,000 viewers participating in the final choice. The digital media age's holy grail – cross-platform, interactive, trendsetting and lucrative – was thus successfully achieved by this glorified game show, and rival networks and production companies looked on enviously at a cross-media event capable of dominating the pop-cultural life of a nation for a whole season.

Between 2001 and 2003 the genre launched with *Expedition Robinson* featured regularly on screens across the world with formats based on novel, subtly different or remarkably similar premises to *Survivor* or *Big Brother*. Reality TV shows such as *Temptation Island* (*Survivor* with a dating/infidelity twist), *The Mole* (*Survivor* with paramilitary adventure-chic), *Eden* (*Big Brother* for teens, with added audience interactivity), *Shipwrecked* (*Survivor* for teens), *The Amazing Race* (*Survivor*, cross-country, against the clock), *Fear Factor* (*Survivor* challenges with extreme sports twist), *Cruel Winter* (*Fear Factor* mixed with *Big Brother*, for the kids), *Road Rules* (*The Amazing Race* with teens in cars), *Lost* (*The Amazing Race*), *Love Cruise* (*Big Brother* and *Survivor* on a boat), *Castaway* (*Survivor* in the cold, without the challenges), and *Murder in Small Town X*, *Chained*, *The Chair*, *The Chamber*, *The Human Zoo*, the marvellously named but barely watchable *I'm A Celebrity . . . Get Me Out Of Here!* and others too minor or awful to elaborate on spread across networks and nations. Everywhere there were storms of protest from the quality press, and drool from ratings-hungry network executives. Concerns were raised in many quarters for the well-being of contestants exposed to the ever-present eye of the camera and a plethora of bizarre settings, endurance tests and production-side manipulations. Condemned, adored and often the subject of litigation, reality TV was the ratings event of the young century.

Across nations, reaction to *Big Brother* amongst the intelligentsia was predictably outraged. The *New Yorker* exhorted its readers not to watch the show. The Russian Orthodox Church called *Za Steklom*, the Russian mutation of *Big Brother*, 'depraved', stating in an open letter to the national networks, 'It is highly probable that participation in this program will have a long-term negative impact on the personal development, family and intimate relations of the young people who are behind the glass.' In Turkey, the Radio and Television Supreme Board ordered the Turkish *Big Brother* mutation, *Someone is Watching Us*, off the air. *Le Monde* excoriated *Loft Story*, the French twist on the format, on its front page over three consecutive days, and Pope John Paul II denounced the show. Much of the cultural criticism concentrates on the brand of fame the shows thrive off and generate. Or rather, not fame, but celebrity, 'being famous

for being famous'. The targets are the producers, the media
culture that feeds off the shows, the audience and, not least,
the contestants who find themselves fodder for an age-old
debate about the worth and nature of fame in the modern
age. This argument, which naturally roves across subjects
and is often applied, particularly in Britain, to the
responsibilities and standards of television to its susceptible
public, has naturally coalesced around reality television as a
suitable ground on which to fight for cultural values.

This explains much of Salman Rushdie's ire when he
criticised reality television in a widely syndicated article:

> The television set, once so idealistically thought of as our
> window on the world, has become a dime-store mirror
> instead. Who needs images of the world's rich otherness,
> when you can watch these half-familiar avatars of yourself –
> these half-attractive half-persons – enacting ordinary life
> under weird conditions? Who needs talent, when the una-
> shamed self-display of the talentless is constantly on offer?[2]

Rushdie is not only deploring one genre of light entertainment – the culture at large is responsible, he implies,
for creating and perpetuating a society in which these
things, these empty values, the cyclical consumption of
'half-familiar avatars' of ourselves, are seen as worthy of
attention. The genre attracted many similar critiques, most
clustering around *Big Brother* rather than the other early
flagship *Survivor*, which looked, and was, more expensive,

---

2. 'Reality TV: a dearth of talent and the death of morality', *Guardian*, 9 June
   2001.

with a narrative that built and climaxed along lines closer to conventional drama. The highbrow commentators as one threw up their arms in bewilderment: *Why are we watching this?* 'Reality', filtered, packaged and marketed, has proven itself to be the most controversial product going.

Of course, 'reality TV' is something of an oxymoron, and the term does not hold up to scrutiny. The genre never sought to portray real life, and most producers are open about the intrinsically selective nature of the editing process, and the artificiality of the situations in which contestants are filmed. It is about 'reality' only inasmuch as it features neither actors nor scripts. The casts are composed of non-actors, their dialogue unscripted, but it's only as real as anything can be in a TV studio, or inside an elaborate island-based game show. 'Reality TV' is a catchy description more handy for gossip columns and water-cooler conversation than 'various kinds of unscripted entertainment involving members of the public'. It is a catch-all term, a convenient shorthand for many kinds of television. *Big Brother*, *Survivor* and their many emulators represent the culmination of a long history of 'reality programming', using non-specialist actors to frame action around. In the US, shows such as *Who Wants To Be A Millionaire?* and *The Weakest Link* are often spoken of as reality TV shows, while in Europe they're thought of as straight quiz shows. Talk shows, too, are reality programming of a kind, and docusoaps, which swarmed over schedules in the nineties, had roots in documentary. As any genre does, this one bleeds at the edges.

For our purposes, we concentrate for the most part on the kind of reality TV that might best be described as the 'reality game shows' such as *Survivor*, *Big Brother* and their imitators. Through these, one can best chart the changing nature of the global television industry, and focus on spectacles of extremity and cruelty never previously produced in the name of light entertainment. In them, several strands meet – the fetishisation of the ordinary, the elevation of the personal and interpersonal to the level of grand narrative, the exploitation of the real subjects who consent to appear in the shows, and the involvement of professionals who confer legitimacy on the form while neglecting the real dangers and ethical problems that their involvement raises. By manufacturing gameworlds into which they slot their non-actor casts, creating pressurised and untested environments, where people are manipulated in cruel and extreme ways and begin to display the confusion and loss of perspective of the incarcerated, these productions use their power without adequate or sufficiently transparent checks and safeguards. As such, reality TV is ripe for a critical examination. Considerations of space prevent us from examining many shows in detail, and it has been necessary to prioritise certain genres of reality game show above others. As such, little reference is made in these pages to the audition game shows such as *Popstars*, *Pop Idol*, *American Idol* and *Fame Academy*. More than any other reality shows, these are no more than an old television formula – the audition/ variety show – repackaged with turn-of-the-century glitz and production techniques learned from *Big Brother* et al.

The authors concede that the success of these shows in ratings terms might make such an omission seem curious; in truth, however, there is nothing of great interest to be said about such programmes – and even less about the 'music' that results from them.

There are many discourses about reality and its representations, and post-modern theory makes it impossible to posit such a thing as a sole objective reality, a first, *a priori* point from which reality's representations fray and refract. Rather, there are many realities, none unproblematic, reality and its representations caught in endless reflections of each other. This given, we seek to avoid such wranglings here, and to concentrate on the productions themselves. Rather than unpick the many threads of assumption contained in its weave, we're content to leave 'reality TV' as a mucky, inadequate term. Sign and signifier merrily slip and slide all over each other, but we leave the semiotics to others – the story, bizarre and bumpy ride though it is, can still be told.

The following chapter is broadly historical, an account of the forerunners to the reality game shows. The conception and rise of these gameworlds, particularly the original big two, *Survivor* and *Big Brother*, and an interpretation of the commercial pressures that led to their imitation on a massive scale, are the subjects of the third chapter, Format Wars.

In the second half of the book we develop an argument about what takes place inside the gameworlds, examining their interior through the lens of psychology. We examine

how contestants are exposed to conditions that can undermine their own sense of reality and personal identity, their
feelings and perceptions manipulated with tools borrowed
from other, sinister areas of life – from psychological
interrogation techniques to the situationist social psychology experiments of the 1960s and early 1970s, which, like
the reality game shows, took public citizens as their
experimental subjects.

Our cast of characters is made up of a host of contestants,
TV producers, psychologists, analysts, academics and other
media professionals. Thanks go to all those, named and
unnamed in these pages, who talked to us, gave us inside
information, and otherwise helped to open up for examination these recent, energetic, avaricious, market-
changing, people-consuming, irascible, cruel, often secretive
and sometimes spectacularly grotesque gameworlds.

2

FORERUNNERS

The term 'reality TV' entered general usage in the early 1990s, when a succession of programmes based on footage of emergency service personnel, such as Fox's long-running *Cops*, became a regular fixture on primetime schedules. The genre spread quickly, and diversified into a range of specialist forms, eventually to culminate in the reality game shows *Survivor* and *Big Brother*. In the case of both the emergency-service-based shows and the later game show genre, the programmes were packaged by their makers, and for the most part accepted by the press, as definitively 'new'. These, the public was informed, were programmes whose use of 'real people' (as opposed to actors) in unscripted situations made them different from any earlier form of television. In the case of the reality game shows, it seemed amnesia had set in, for they incited many of the same debates, allegations of encouraging voyeurism with the peddling of 'trash TV', that had been heard before, in reference to *Cops* and its imitators. In both cases the rhetoric of novelty was overstated, for the genres owed a great deal to earlier kinds of film and television. The constructed scenarios of *Survivor* and *Big Brother*, like those of the pro-grammes that were to follow them, do represent a new hybrid form, but the hyperbolic declarations that television had carved out new territory for itself with this explicit focus on 'the real' were disingenuous. Indeed, by the time *Big Brother* went on screen in Holland it had been some seventy-five years since filmmakers first declared their intention of screening 'the real'. It was not 'reality' that was new in all this, but what producers chose to understand by it – a very different 'reality' from that which had first drawn the attention of filmmakers, and laid the groundwork, technically and rhetorically, for the genre that was to be known as reality TV. This chapter will chart the relation-ship between film, television and 'the real', seeking to discover just what was truly new about the wave of reality that crashed around the world from the early 1990s onwards.

French, Lies and Videotape

The relationship between film and notions of 'the real' can be traced back to 1839, when the French National Assembly acquired the daguerreotype patents 'for the world' at the behest of the radical deputy François Arago. In making his appeal to the representatives of the French people, Arago emphasised the scientific applications of the camera, citing such examples of its potential as 'making accurate copies of hieroglyphics, and, more generally, for physicists and meteorologists'.[3] Arago compared the camera to the thermometer, barometer and microscope, as an instrument of scientific measurement which could serve the pursuit of objective knowledge. The photograph was assumed to be pure as an evidentiary object, free from the bias of eyewitness accounts. The consequences of Arago's rhetoric have been far-reaching, for, in claiming the camera for science, he established a general perception of photography that continues to this day. The widespread belief that cameras cannot – or at least, for the most part, do not – lie reflects Arago's conviction that the camera was a weapon for the scientific arsenal, as opposed to an artist's tool. The camera, as a mechanical (or electronic) 'eye' was understood to do no more than capture images of the world, and this understanding has proved remarkably durable.

Ninety years on from Arago's intervention, film had been put to some distinctly unscientific purposes, and the moving picture industry was well on its way to becoming the international behemoth that defined so much of the twentieth century. Hollywood had seized upon film as an entertainment medium, and cinemas around the world screened a constant stream of newsreels and features. In Britain, John Grierson, a philosophy graduate from Glasgow University, reacted with disgust to what he saw as the new film industry's trivial fixation on glamour and dramatic cliché. Grierson resolved to use film as a medium of public

---

3. Brian Winston, *Claiming the Real: The Documentary Film Revisited*, British Film Institute Publishing, 1995.

education. The first recorded use of the term 'documentary', in a 1926 film review, is attributed to Grierson. His coining of the term (in reference to film) was controversial. Indeed, virtually all who expressed an opinion about the term were scathing. Pare Lorentz, an early American documentarist, swore it gave him migraines, while Alberto Cavalcanti, Grierson's influential sound man,[4] said it 'smelt of dust and boredom'.[5] Nonetheless, the term entered professional and later public language, if only because no better alternative could be found.

If the term 'documentary' was unpopular and dull, Grierson's definition of the medium as 'the creative treatment of actuality' made things worse; it remains a matter of debate just what he meant, and attempts at explanation have confused things further. 'Actuality', a synonym for 'reality', is straightforward enough at first glance, but 'creative treatment' would seem to suggest that 'reality' in the documentary is less than 'pure', as it undergoes the mediation of 'creativity'. To some extent, Grierson was seeking to distinguish his medium from the merely journalistic dimensions of the newsreel, which he saw as a rather vapid form given to the 'news' of gossip and society babbling (bear in mind the classic newsreel images of bicycling chimpanzees). The 'actuality', or 'reality' that Grierson sought to address, by contrast, was avowedly serious.

Spoken of as the founder of the realist tradition in

---

4. Ibid.
5. Ibid.

documentary, Grierson claimed that his use of film was incidental. It was not his intention, he argued, primarily to be a filmmaker – rather, film was the best medium with which to pursue the goal of public education. The curriculum he wished to serve was that of sociological enlightenment, and classic Griersonian documentaries such as the 1936 *Housing Problems* were closely wedded to a reformist political agenda. In his own words, written in 1942:

> We were reformers, open and avowed: Concerned – to use the old jargon – with 'bringing alive the new materials of citizenship', 'crystallising sentiments' and creating those 'new loyalties from which a progressive civic will might derive. Take that away and I'd be hard put to it to say what I have been working for these past fifteen years.[6]

Although Grierson avoided identifying himself with any political party, his rhetoric was that of the democratic left. Documentary, in his eyes, was to be used to enlighten the masses to the circumstances of their society, in the expectation that such knowledge would enable them to bring pressure to bear upon their governments for social reform. This was not to be done, however, by the merely informative techniques of journalism – documentary's 'creative treatment' of the real, manifested in the use of such devices as interview to camera, music and the cameraman's usual bag of tricks, marked it as a more ambitious medium. It sought to present social facts, build a case and present an argument. Grierson maintained that these arguments were

---

6. Forsyth Hardy, ed., *Grierson on Documentary*, Faber and Faber, 1966.

reformist, 'openly' and 'avowedly'; in other words, he aimed to make the empirical case for social democracy. This understanding of the purpose and potential of film was very much a product of its time, and the contemporaneous belief than an enlightened citizenry was an essential bulwark against the twin threats of fascism and revolutionary communism. Combined with the impression of profound political danger confronting the West was a faith in the masses couched in condescending language. Grierson ended the essay quoted above with the words: 'deep down, the people want to be fired to tougher ways of thought and feeling. In that habit they will win more than a war.'[7]

This reading of Grierson has been challenged, most notably by Brian Winston, in his *Claiming the Real: The Documentary Film Revisited*. Winston argues that Grierson's professional circumstances, as a filmmaker initially employed by the general post office, and later a variety of government agencies, made the achievement of his stated aims impossible. With the exception of the period 1929–31, all the Griersonian government films were commissioned by Conservative administrations, and this funding situation prevented the production of radical documentaries. Moreover, Winston argues that the 'creativity' quotient in the equation was rather more evident than the actuality – the contextualised 'social meaning' of such phenomena as poverty and urban blight could not be communicated in the documentary form, with its inherent

---

7. Ibid.

focus upon particularities. The revisionist interpretation of Grierson, which finds a large gap between his rhetorical claims and the films he produced, suggests that even when the filmmaker is determined to address his subjects in the full light of their social meaning, limitations of both form and funding can rob the project of success. Grierson's writings on the documentary, however, were as influential as, if not more influential than, his films. The Griersonian creed, however compromised, was one of commitment and engagement. The project may have failed, but its formulation was to leave a legacy that did much to define the practice of later filmmakers, and was transferred to television by Griersonians such as Paul Rotha. When Grierson wrote that 'if there is one thing that good propaganda must not do these days it is to give people catharsis', he staked out an ambitious preserve for the documentary: it was to toughen and arm the people with an understanding of their world that would spur them on to action. The people, for their part, were unconvinced, and overwhelmingly uninterested.

The Griersonian documentary, often referred to as 'expository', was concerned with the construction of an argument, described in Jon Dovey's *Freakshow: First Person Media and Factual Television*[8] as issuing from a 'we the filmmakers to a we the public'. The narrative standpoint in such films owes much to traditional modes of twentieth-century academic discourse, where the 'objective' philoso-

---

8. Pluto Press, 2000.

pher or historian writes from the 'God's-eye view'. Their arguments issue from an apparently impersonal standpoint, with the author making no reference to the fact of their own subjectivity. Such modes have been heavily criticised as a 'sleight of hand', where, by adopting a conventional form of address intended to minimise authorial bias, subjectivity is excluded from appearance in the text. As subjective considerations, though hidden, still exist, this can be seen as a professional conceit that simply denies the troublesome issue of all parties having but a single pair of eyes, which, unlike the idealised camera, are all too capable of lying, to themselves and others both.

Such an argumentative standpoint is described by Dovey as corresponding to a period in which objectivity was considered possible, prior to the confounding doubts of post-modern philosophies and the breakdown of ideology. Bill Nichols has described the documentary in this mould as a 'discourse of sobriety', akin to politics, science, economics and foreign policy: 'Discourses of sobriety are sobering because they regard their relation to the real as direct, immediate, transparent. Through them power exerts itself. Through them, things are made to happen. They are the vehicles of domination and conscience, power and knowledge, desire and will.'[9] Nichols notes that 'documentary, despite its kinship, has never been accepted as a full equal'. Equal, that is, of politics, economics, et cetera, whose capacity to affect the world is undeniable. While

---

9. *Introduction to Documentary*, Indiana University Press, 2000.

such acceptance was withheld from documentarists, they sought for generations to achieve it. This led to a fulfilment of Cavalcanti's olfactory prophecy – the word 'documentary' and the films produced as such did seem to strike the viewing public as 'dust and boredom'. The serious, sober documentary could not compete, when screened in the cinema, with the intoxicated outpourings of Hollywood, and when transplanted to television fared as badly against drama and light entertainment. Although Grierson's rhetoric shaped television's regard for the documentary and guaranteed its place as the most worthy and prestigious of genres, the baggage of 'boredom' and 'condescending' modes of address relegated it to a position of unpopularity. The documentary survived on television owing to the public service commitment of early broadcasting. Nonetheless, primetime documentaries were always a rarity, and the 'ghettoisation' of documentary in low audience slots became one of its most consistent features. This was to change in Britain in the 1990s when the documentary was put to purposes and subjects very different from Grierson's, but with this exception, the documentary was, for all the critical attention and praise it won, a medium best known for its ability to make an audience change channels. If the people did desire 'tougher ways of thought and feeling', they were suppressing the urge.

From Exposition to Vérité: The 'Abandonment of Argument'

The Griersonian documentary and its rationalisations became embedded in the public service culture of British broadcasting, and exerted wide international influence. Aspiring documentarists pledged themselves to the cause of public education, leading, inevitably, to the perception that the worthy documentary, with its didacticism and avowed seriousness, was something for the chattering classes to nod over and emote with – but not something to be much enjoyed. In time, technological advances created new opportunities for the documentary filmmaker, and variations on the expository form were launched in a blaze of rhetoric. Most influential in the later development of reality shows were two varieties of documentary that emerged in the 1960s – direct cinema and cinéma-vérité. Showing once again the preponderance of terminological confusion in the field, the terms have been used interchangeably, by both practitioners and critics. For the sake of convenience, here Brian Winston's definitions will be used, 'direct cinema' referring to the American 'fly on the wall' school of Richard Leacock and Frederick Wiseman, and 'cinéma-vérité' to the work of Jean Rouche and his disciples.

Both forms were in part a reaction to the Griersonian confusion over objectivity. For the first time, light, portable cameras were available which allowed for the shooting of synchronous sound. The Griersonians, working in the 1930s, could record sound only via an unwieldy apparatus that filled an entire truck – now, cameras such as the Auricon, and recorders such as the Nagra, granted film-makers a previously unthinkable mobility and flexibility. They also allowed for the presence of a film crew to be far less obtrusive. Grierson's followers had for years been accused of excessive interference with their subjects. Not only did the technology available require them to engage in a good deal of dramatic reconstruction, with synchronous sound no more than a distant dream on location shoots, but interview subjects would be very much aware of the bulky equipment and artificiality of the situation. Direct cinema sought to capture 'actuality' with rather less creative intervention – the camera was to be a passive agent, and, in the more extreme schools, the production team was to avoid even making eye contact with their subjects.

The gold standard of direct cinema was set by films such as D.A. Pennebaker's *Don't Look Back*, on Bob Dylan's 1965 tour of England, and Frederick Wiseman's substantial oeuvre, including the controversial mental hospital of *Titicut Follies*. Seeking to convey 'the feeling of being there', direct cinema did not, in the Griersonian mode, make explicit arguments about its subject – indeed, the proponents of the new technique insisted that the viewers were left to make up their own minds about the film's content. Although interviews still appeared in direct cinema films, they were used as sparingly as possible. The direct cinema camera prefers to follow its subjects around their natural habitat, be it the campaign trail in 1960, captured in Leacock's *Primary*, or the concert halls and hotel rooms of

Don't Look Back. In Pennebaker's words: 'It's possible to go to a situation and simply film what you see there, what happens there, what goes on ... and what's a film? It's just a window someone peeps through.'

These were the scientific claims for the camera repeated. Direct cinema, so Pennebaker claimed, simply put 'a window' in the wall of particular subjects. There was no attempt to analyse or interpret in pedagogic mode. Direct cinema filmmakers such as Richard Leacock went further than Pennebaker, abandoning even the interview as too authorial. Pure direct cinema became the classic, observational 'fly on the wall' standpoint, and, in committing to the discipline of 'not asking anyone to do anything' (Leacock's phrase), positioned itself to make stronger truth-claims than the Griersonian form. After all, if one were merely to point a camera at 'actuality' and offer no interpretation, let alone intervention, what would be left but evidence of a scientific grade?

Closer examination shows the claims made by Pennebaker to be, again, an overstatement of the possibility of directorial self-effacement. Pennebaker's interview with Dylan in *Don't Look Back* was clearly not the act of an objective presence; his terror and adulation of Dylan shine through, even though we never see the director's face. Leacock eschewed the interview as being too contrived, but even such puritanism could not erase the fact of subjectivity. The very act of selecting where one positions Pennebaker's window decides not only what is seen, but what meaning accrues to it. The idea that the inanimate camera could overwhelm the sophistications of subjectivity with mechanical honesty was a myth.

Recognition of this was to be the foundational principle of the 'reflexive' cinéma-vérité of Jean Rouche, in which the filmmaker's presence seeped out from the faux objectivity behind the camera and appeared in-shot. It was Rouche's conviction that the pretence of 'God's-eye view' detachment was a falsehood; the documentary could not be a 'window on the world', as the director's 'frame' was inevitably coloured. The form could, however, provide a window that did not obstruct the view of the filmmakers themselves; by entering the frame and displaying their subjective presence, the documentarist abandoned the traditional pretence of objectivity, allowing for a more equal relationship with their subject.

The impact of direct cinema and cinéma-vérité was far-reaching, as documentarists began to use the fly-on-the-wall perspective on everyday subjects. 1971 saw *An American Family*, followed some years later by Paul Watson's *The Family* in Britain. These films portrayed 'family life' through the lens of singular domestic arrangements, implicitly presented as representing the domestic norm. Social meaning was here addressed not in the analytical/instructive mode of exposition, but through the depiction of the average family's average day. These techniques were to lay the ground for a whole new take on actuality.

Direct cinema owed much to new technology and dissatisfaction with the earlier documentary form, but also reflected broader changes in society. Reaching its zenith in the 1960s, it applied itself eagerly to the everyday, the domestic, and the 'community profile', focusing not on social 'problems' or issues but society and its members, as it were, 'in the raw'. This could be, and was, explained in terms of the shortcomings of the Griersonian method, but those shortcomings were themselves more apparent in the 1960s than a generation before, and yet more so in the decades that followed. The world and the ways it saw itself were changing.

First-Person Primacy: Trivia Goes Primetime

Grierson's doctrine of public enlightenment issued from a time when the notions of 'objectivity' and general truth-claims won tacit acceptance. This world was a place where the grand narratives of ideology, from Marxism–Leninism to social democracy, were sovereign over many lives and minds – reality could be interpreted in the light of tota-lising systems, imposing disinterested and rational order on the trivia of subjectivity. Meaning and truth were proper-ties of the general claim, the overarching system, and the all-encompassing philosophy. That documentary was con-ceived in the light of such an epistemology made the Griersonian form a logical development. But the episte-mology was to buckle beneath an onslaught of changing social and political attitudes, resulting, at last, in a world and sober documentary form that were to become quite intoxicated – with themselves.

In his novel *Atomised*,[10] Michel Houellebecq depicts the 1960s as a period that glorified the self, at the expense of notions of community, class and nation. Post-war prosperity and the social liberalisation that it brought accentuated the importance of subjective desire, and the notion of self-fulfilment as the ultimate goal became the guiding compass of the baby boomer generation. Literature and media of confession began to proliferate, with a tendency to publicise the once-private becoming evident. Feminist autobiographies written in the passionate belief that personal and political were one became bestsellers, while in the US, the talk show began its evolution into the carnival of revelation, eccentricity and absurdity that has since become a global phenomenon. Early docusoaps such as *An American Family* appeared, signifying documentary's first steps away from 'social issues' towards social actors, or, to avoid the jargon, 'real' or 'ordinary' people. Public discourse began alluding to the previously undiscussed, with movements such as Stonewall turning, in Robertson Davies' phrase, 'the love that dare not speak its name' into 'the love that never shuts up'. As personal liberation became a pre-eminent political goal, the first-person voice grew louder and more confident. The politics of the self were to be the most durable and exportable legacy of the American new left.

Jon Dovey, in his *Freakshow: First Person Media and Factual Television*, argues that the spread of media from

10. Vintage, 2001.

confessional autobiography to the talk show and reflexive documentaries was a consequence of the collapse of ideological narratives confronted by the hegemonic force of neoliberalism. The argument, simply, is that the observed failure of traditional ideologies of the left led to the triumph of a new right that both contributed to an ongoing glorification of the self, and undermined communitarian impulses in civic society. This led in turn to an inversion of traditional conceptions of the private and public spheres, as evidenced by works ranging from headlines addressing themselves frankly to Bill Clinton's member, to the intensely personal documentaries of Michael Moore. Once unthinkable works, such as Tracey Emin's *My Boyfriend Fucked Me in the Arse and I Enjoyed It*, represent, in Dovey's view, the logical extremes of this development, and a new regime of truth, in which subjectivity, once derided as a source of personal bias and distortion, becomes instead the essential ground of knowledge. Under this 'regime of truth', a metaphoric speaker wins the belief of their audience not by reference to overarching theory, but to personal experience. To have suffered, experienced, 'been through' things, becomes the foundation of real knowledge. If it doesn't bleed, it can't be trusted.

The works that Dovey refers to are compelling evidence of a changed sensibility, but his explanation appears to ignore the wider cultural field in which they emerged. In attributing the transition to neoliberalism, Dovey assumes the primary determinant of narrative standpoint to be the popularity of competing political visions. While it is unquestionable that neoliberalism, with its focus upon personal wealth, has enforced a rugged – and inconsistent – individualism, invoking it as a transcendent entity that has single-handedly swept the world that was before it over-looks other powerful influences. Away from the terrain of the conventionally political, a new movement was to impact upon the disengaged children of the Thatcher and Reagan eras, laying the groundwork for the coming of reality TV – and much besides.

Ideologies of Liberation and the New Domains of Selfhood

It has become a cliché to refer to the last century as 'Freudian', but by the 1970s, the domination of psy-chotherapeutic and psychiatric practice by psychoanalysis was on the wane in the US, while in much of Europe psychoanalysis proper had always been the preserve of very few. An unassuming breed of psychotherapy outpaced the factionalised and overpriced analysts, reinforcing the poli-tics of the self and validating personal experience as the grounding of knowledge. The inoffensive, and superficially benign creeds of humanistic psychology, above all the counselling of Carl Rogers, were reaching a far larger constituency than the analysts ever had, and their ideas, such as they were, found numerous echoes in the personal liberation movement. By its insistence that the analysts were wrong to tinker with the subconscious with their arcane theoretical tools, counselling validated the conscious mind, the intentional choice and individual autonomy. As Rogers puts it: 'I can trust my experience ... evaluation by others is not a guide for me'.[11] With professed roots in existentialism, humanistic psychology prioritises individual experience above all else, and is unambiguous in its epistemological claims. All real knowledge is a product of personal experience, and the counsellors' role merely to create a space in which persons can speak freely, thus coming to an understanding of the experiences they should trust. The counsellor is no more than a facilitator, bringing no dogma to the face-to-face session (clients are counselled from a sedentary, rather than horizontal, position). The goal of therapy is for the client to attain belief in the inherent value and positive nature of their experience, to be able to say with Rogers, 'evaluation by others is not a guide for me'.

Counselling remains the most popular form of psychotherapy, but its influence extends far beyond the confines of those who practise or receive it. The wackier shores of psychotherapy were built on the foundations of the humanistic schools; from EST (Erhard Seminars Training, a much mocked but profitable movement in its time), to 'rebirthing' and countless sub-varieties of group and individual therapy, the explosion in the 1970s and 1980s of new, non-medical and functionally cretinous schools of

---

11. 'This is me', in Howard Kirschenbaum, ed., *Carl Rogers Reader*, Constable, 1990.

psychological healing paid lip service to the anodyne and solipsistic message of counselling. The inner search, the drive to 'truly become oneself', is immersed in the rhetoric that Rogers perfected in La Jolla and the University of Chicago counselling school; the self-help industries, with their earth tone language of 'authenticity' and self-exploration, are rooted in the same reification of sovereign subjectivity. Wedding the 1960s ethos of self-gratification to an unfalteringly positive view of human nature, Rogers, though thought of as an American left-liberal, created the cultural corollary of new right economic doctrines, one that could prosper even where the Chicago School's curves and longing to castrate inflation found no welcome. The message that selfhood was the source of truth and meaning was avidly received by the baby boomers and their children, seeping out from the halls of group therapy and cheap paperbacks into the sprawling self-obsession now so omnipresent as to go unnoticed.

On television, this was evident in a variety of first-person media, from the docusoap (see below), whose only contents are a workplace or domestic setting and its inhabitants, to the confessional and explicitly therapeutic American talk show, where the most personal of experiences are proudly trumpeted to an audience that cheers or jeers each statement. *My experience is valid, of inherent interest, indeed inherent truth.* There is no church, as one of Irvine Welsh's more drug-damaged characters puts it, but the church of the self.[12]

---

12. *The Acid House*, Vintage, 1995.

This first-person primacy, the detritus of burgeoning industries that proffer happiness and fulfilment, has entered deep into the culture and minds that comprise it. The 'real people' featured in docusoaps and reality game shows, given to lengthy first-person monologues and references to 'formative experience', the 'I am' statements that abound in an America long immersed in self-help literature, have internalised the navel-gazing focus on the smallest facts of selfhood. The first person thus raised to the status of sole truth, sole value and sole source of narrative makes few allusions to things beyond its boundaries; other selves and their inherent interest are acknowledged, indeed, the private group is a crucial space for the interplay of selves, but notions of community, polity and public space are distant background to the revels of a subjectivity that is its own reward and kingdom. This does not necessarily manifest itself in blatant self-obsession, with the baggage of high-octane emotion and confessional tones. Indeed, a more striking consequence of first-person primacy in reality TV is the focus upon trivial, everyday behaviour, from static shots of contestants cutting toenails or playing with their hair to 'God's voice commentary' on the preparation of meals or conflict over shopping budgets in *Big Brother*. This dandruff of selfhood, elevated to the status of a worthy subject, rushes in to fill the space vacated by overarching narratives that once extended the range of their followers' vision, however imperfectly, beyond the little facts of individual existence. There is no aspect of personal experience too small to fix a camera on – trivia, indeed, is the new rock'n'roll.

Trivial Pursuits and the 'Salvation' of the Documentary

By 1998, the British documentary was in serious trouble. The public service culture, which had ensured its prominence in weekly schedules despite the meagre ratings it attracted, was all but dead, a victim of deregulation. Increased competition had not led to a greater variety of programming – indeed, it had enforced an ethos of ever greater imitation, as producers battled for audience share in a contracting, volatile market. The traditional documentary, with its slow, expository pace and intensity of focus, was not the kind of programming that attracted much by way of advertising revenues. At Channel 4, once the spiritual home of serious documentary, a generation of commissioning editors were replaced, in the words of a former producer and one-time Emmy winner 'by a bunch of bloody twelve-year-olds'. These pre-pubescents, described by the same source as 'snot-nosed bastards', though for the most part Oxbridge-educated and in a very establishment mould, had been raised on a different kind of television than their forebears. They understood how to appeal to a youthful audience, and were shameless in their populism. The 'worthy' documentary of old was not something that they cared for. Budgets shrank, and a generation of documentary filmmakers now in their forties and fifties, who had done much to build Channel 4's reputation, were forced to bite their tongues as the twelve-year-olds asked in all innocence – 'So what is it that you do, exactly?'

To make things worse, there were a series of scandals over 'faked' documentaries, perceived as having used reconstruction and altered chronology to create false impressions. In the wake of a Carlton documentary on Colombian drug cartels, which proposed the worrying but factually challenged theory that a flood of cheap South American heroin was on its way to British streets, the *Guardian* newspaper began a major investigation, and established that the film, by award-winning producer Mark Beaufort, was substantially a fabrication. Famously, a dramatic sequence purporting to show a mule en route from Bogotá to London with a stomach full of smack was exposed as fiction. The 'mule's' ticket had been bought with Beaufort's American Express card, there was no proof that the powder he swallowed was heroin, and several Colombian interviewers claimed to be members of the Cali cartel were nothing of the kind. There had already been something of a scandal over a Channel 4 documentary's use of reconstruction, when a film on builders, *Rogue Males*, was shown to have set up a crucial scene presented as spontaneous. Carlton were fined two million pounds for the 'connection' affair, and ominous voices warned that the documentary's day was done. In the face of declining ratings and a public service culture of broadcasting that had been eviscerated by the long years of Thatcherism, it seemed the form was destined to retreat further into late-night slots, a curiosity for the ageing and jaded. If, deep down, the people wanted to be fired to tougher ways of thought and feeling, they were keeping it to themselves.

At the very moment that the documentary looked all but dead, a renaissance of sorts began. 'Of sorts', because the documentary form that was to achieve the unheard of, displacing soap operas and drama from the primetime schedules, winning massive audience shares, was a very different creature from the sombre products of direct cinema. All the conventional rhetoric of documentary fell away, as the form discovered a sense of humour, and learned to glory in the trivial.

Sylvania Waters, broadcast in 1993, occasioned the first recorded use of the term 'docusoap'. The series was an observational profile of an Australian family, who had admitted a film crew to their home for six months, in the understanding that they could be filmed at all times 'except when in the bathroom or making love'. The executive producer, Paul Watson, was not new to the observational form; in 1974, he had filmed *The Family*, a twelve-part, much praised series on an 'ordinary' British clan from Reading. Like its stateside predecessor, 1971's *An American Family*, Watson's film attracted a good deal of press commentary, and proved more successful than the apparently less-than-promising subject matter, the 'ordinaries', suggested possible. Watson made his reputation with *The Family*, and continued to make occasional observational films through the 1980s, but while his work was well received, it did not, until the 1990s, set the schedules on fire.

As the 1990s got under way, the TV establishment was ready for the form. Commissioning editors had for some

time been saying that they wanted character-based documentaries with plot lines. Watson's work had established an
effective and straightforward technique for the translation
of methods associated with drama to the documentary form.
Docusoaps take a number of 'characters', social actors performing themselves, and follow them through their days (or
weeks, or months), intercutting several stories per episode
in the manner of a soap opera. While soap opera plots
might proceed around high-tension personal confrontations, revelations of infidelity or personal crisis, the 'drama'
quotient in the docusoap is low. Most locations are work-
place-orientated, the characters going about their daily
lives, and while many are inclined to 'perform' for the
camera, caricaturing themselves with exuberant humour,
the settings and 'storylines' are often banal. Nonetheless,
the form was a smash hit.

In 1999, the BBC had no less than twelve docusoaps in
various stages of production. From *Driving School* to *Animal
Hospital*, *Airport* to *Babewatch*, their settings were everyday,
and, to many critics, tedious. In its selection of subject
matter, the docusoap traduced the traditional logic of
documentary, for docusoaps have no 'subject' in the sense of
being 'about' anything. No serious attempt is made to
inform, and Griersonian influence is conspicuous by its
absence. The docusoap refers to nothing outside the narrow
confines of its location; it zeroes in on 'social actors', displaying the day-to-day exigencies of their lives, and in
several cases making stars of them. Maureen Rees became a
national heroine on the back of her appearances in *Driving*

School, while crooner Jane MacDonald of nautical docusoap *The Cruise* signed with EMI and recorded a successful album on the back of her new celebrity.

The docusoap serves up a purview of life on a cruise ship, in a shopping mall, takes viewers further into worlds they have passed through in person; it does not analyse, interpret, or indeed do anything but point a camera and add a line or two of scene-setting 'God's voice' commentary. Here was an unquestionable slice of 'actuality', although the customary debates about mediation took place again; docusoap producers, like all documentarists, might play with chronology and indulge in various forms of manipulation, but not the kinds that result in seven-figure fines. It was difficult to see much 'creativity' in the treatment of it, however; the form proscribed much more than passivity on the part of the production team, save when footage was dull enough to necessitate some pacing in the edit. For the most part, the equal duration of all scenes resulted in a curious constancy; everything was given the same time and space, no character receiving particular emphasis or shading.

Brian Winston has explained the success of the docusoap in terms of its inversion of public expectations of the documentary. There are moments, he argues, rare and unpredictable, when by a combination of circumstance and blind chance, a genre reaches beyond its usual boundaries and subverts itself with the introduction of unfamiliar elements. In the case of the docusoap, the X factor was humour, not considered an important – if even a decent –

aspect of documentary. The associative nexus of the word 'documentary' itself, 'worthy', 'dull', 'intelligent' and 'serious' programming, was blown away by the docusoaps' fixation on the trivial, the everyday and ordinary. Moreover, the many instances of workplace humour and banter made for light, engaging viewing. The public responded to this sudden metamorphosis with new enthusiasm.

It was a depressing spectacle for the Griersonian. If the documentary 'call to arms', the urge to display actuality in order to change it, had never been successful, it had at least remained a high ambition. The docusoap represented its final abandonment. Nothing in *The Cruise* or *Animal Hospital* would incite anyone to write to their MP or Congressperson – there was nothing to see but cruise ships and animals. The form was a repudiation of social purpose and social meaning. Documentary's final popularity had been achieved at the cost of jettisoning the genre's sobriety in favour of a relaxed basking in gossip and banality. It is difficult to conceive of narratives less grand, more particular, than those of the docusoap, which seem superficial when compared not only to the documentary but the soap opera aspect of its composition. As Dovey notes, British soaps often confront social issues, from drugs to teenage pregnancy and homosexuality, and the more popular series seem almost to consider it a compulsory public service function. The docusoap, by contrast, has no truck with issues.

The eschewal of context and significance appears only to have increased the popular appeal of the docusoap.

Although a 'fly on the wall' form, the docusoap embedded a great but inoffensive vanity in its core, a first-person primacy explicit in each character's accession to the proposition that they too could be stars, and need not, in assuming such status, offer any justification of achievement or ability. Here were self-contained worlds of nowhere-in-particular, untroubling eye-candy that revelled in formal simplicity. It was said in defence of the genre that at least documentary had been saved from oblivion, but the manner of its survival left many producers feeling that a clean death would have been preferable.

Reality Unbound:
Surveillance Makes its Mark

In the US, the docusoap took a half-step towards what's now known as reality TV in 1992, when MTV, the idiot child/marketing genius of world airwaves, struck upon the notion of recruiting a young household to populate a loft in Manhattan and conduct their lives before the cameras. It was a very MTV idea, one that allowed them to display their target audience *to* their target audience, in a logical extension of the channel's 'lifestyle branding', portrayed by Naomi Klein as the strategic incubation of a homogenous global youth culture, the better to consume MTV products. *The Real World* went beyond the purely observational technique of the docusoap, creating a setting for the lives it viewed, although participants continued to work and socialise in the outside world. As new seasons were produced, casting techniques were refined to create obvious points of conflict (e.g., recruiting an opinionated young Republican and a HIV-infected gay rights activist to the same household), and locations varied from major US cities to cross-country trips, and, in one case, London. The show made use of 'video diary' segments, with participants delivering first-person monologues to the camera, a technique later enshrined in the major reality game shows.

Before MTV's *The Real World*, another window on the real had already been exported from the US, the genre of emergency-service reality TV typified by Fox's long-running *Cops*. *Cops* takes as its subject police on the beat, following them on call-outs and in confrontations with petty criminals. Immediately branded 'tabloid TV', the show and its many later imitators depict real-world crime in strikingly simple terms, as a conflict between good, wisecracking cops and evil urban lowlifes. The social context of crime is not addressed, any more than the docusoap contextualises its subjects, but the resulting footage has a darker tone than workplace humour. By neglecting the role of poverty in the production of criminality, *Cops* portrays crime as a straightforward matter of individual deviance, rightly arrested by virtuous agents of the law.[13] The resulting drama makes for gripping viewing, but its depiction of crime addresses social meaning rather less thoroughly than comic books, and in its exclusive focus on

---

13. See Dovey, *Freakshow: First Person Media and Factual Television* for a comprehensive, and chilling, elaboration of this argument.

the deviant criminal and their deserved punishment has a certain resonance with new right conceptions of criminality which address themselves solely to the criminal's responsibility for their actions, refusing to consider the social genesis of crime.

Two major studies have been conducted into the appeal of this form of reality TV. In 1992, Mary Beth Oliver and G. Blake Armstrong interviewed 358 American viewers of true crime shows *Cops*, *America's Most Wanted*, *American Detective*, *Top Cops* and *FBI: The Untold Story*. Their research involved the use of a number of psychological questionnaires designed to measure authoritarianism, racial prejudice and predisposition towards criminality, before interrogating viewers on their experience of television. The findings were stark. Aficionados of the true crime shows were overwhelmingly white males with high levels of authoritarianism and racism, who took pleasure in the dramatic arrest footage.[14] Such attitudes were found to be irrelevant in the enjoyment of fictional crime shows, suggesting that the packaging of these programmes, with its emphasis upon the 'real' nature of the footage, spoke directly to an audience hungry to see the underclass taking punishment.

By contrast, a British Film Institute sponsored study conducted by Annette Hill in the UK found that the audience of *Children's Hospital* and other medical-based

---

14. Mary Beth Oliver and G. Blake Armstrong, 'Predictors of viewing and enjoyment of reality-based and fictional crime shows', *Journalism and Mass Communication Quarterly*, vol. 72, no. 3, Autumn 1995.

shows reported a distinctly 'uplifting' and 'moving' viewing experience. Cautioning that viewers showed awareness of press criticisms that the shows pandered to voyeurism, Hill points out that the sample's insistence on the shows as 'uplifting' may be in part a rationalisation of tastes they find shameful in themselves. However, it was clear that viewers took pleasure in witnessing the build-up of tension and eventual release when, for example, a child was followed through the preparation for surgery to successful recovery. Also striking were attitudes towards the doctors and nurses featured in the shows, frequently described as 'caring', 'heroic' and 'noble'. The perceived selflessness and commitment of medical personnel rendered them, in the eyes of many viewers, a breathing personification of public-spiritedness and virtue: 'The depiction of ordinary heroes who work within the medical profession encourages viewers to feel a vicarious civic duty ... this positive portrayal of healthcare and emergency services assured many viewers that they live in a caring society.'[15] In both cases, the findings suggest that the term 'reality TV' belies the shows' less-than-frank portrayal of the societies in which they're based. The Britain of the 1990s saw continuing decline in public services and the introduction of private finance into socialised medicine. In short, the 'caring face' displayed in medical-based reality shows was a pipe dream.

In similarly fantastic vein, Mary Beth Oliver found that

---

15. Annette Hill, 'Fearful and safe', Conference paper, 'Breaking the boundaries', University of Stirling, 29–31 January 1999.

criminality on *Cops* and other shows of its kind bore little resemblance to its real-world counterpart. The shows' need for melodrama led to a disproportionate focus on violent crime, which accounts for some 13 per cent of reported offences in the US, and a staggering 87 per cent of the crimes featured in a 56.5 hour selection from *Cops*, et cetera. Violent as the streets may be in this fantasy preserve, crime doesn't pay; whereas police off-camera solve 18 per cent of reported cases, their primetime avatars do rather better, clearing an impressive 61.5 per cent. The caring, rough and authoritarian realities in these shows have more in common with the worldview of a right-wing Conservative than the actuality of the phenomena they purportedly display. In the case of the hospital shows, this may be misleading, but the mirage of an angelic medical profession, served up as cheap catharsis, is unlikely to supercede viewers' own experience of the National Health Service. In the case of the crime shows it would seem that darker impulses are catered to – and the resulting picture of crime not only overstates the prevalence of violence by a massive factor, but conforms to a simplistic and pernicious view of criminality, embodied in the policy sphere by such measures as 'three strikes and you're out' laws. 'Actuality', observed and recorded with the simplest of techniques, turned out to be a ready bearer of reactionary lies.

The Road to *Survivor*

These acontextual forms provided a frame that neatly encapsulated first-person primacy, premiering elements that would emerge in the hybrid mix of reality game shows. Away from television, the ubiquity of CCTV cameras across much of Europe, and to a lesser extent the States, contributed to a general acceptance of surveillance, while, on the web, the personal surveillance camera, picking up on the 1980s popularity of amateur, video-shot porn, was installed in the bedrooms of various young women, first and most famously that of Jennifer Rigley ('Jennicam'). This development of peeping-tom technology, besides creating for Ms Rigley and others what may well be the stupidest career opportunity of all time, added to the growing potential for taking surveillance into the home, or indeed, anywhere one might choose, for the purposes of entertainment. This had applications far beyond pornography, but the journey to their realisation was a long one. 'Actuality', shorn of social meaning, had market value, but it would require the best efforts of entertainment professionals to package it for sale. On the outer reaches of cutting-edge TV, such efforts had begun in the late 1980s. The next chapter charts their realisation in the ground-breaking reality shows of the late 1990s, that moved yet further from social meaning into the territory of 'social experiments', embracing formal aims so far from Grierson's civic-minded call to arms as to seem the product of a very different species.

3

FORMAT WARS

> The inventor of reality TV? No, but I consider myself to be the pioneering producer who took documentary into a controlled environment and created a new kind of television.
> – Charlie Parsons, originator of *Survivor*.[16]

It took as long to get the format right as it does to make a feature film, from treatment through to fundraising, all the way to final cut. Once finished, it had to be sold, and the very novelty and scale that would make *Survivor* the American TV event of 2000 also made it a difficult show to pitch; at first glance, no one quite knew what it was. For Charlie Parsons, there has always been a bitter-sweet aspect to his format's success. Although the most popular reality game show in the US, it has never achieved the same status in his native Britain, and Parsons, having created an international, award-winning hit, is now semi-detached from the television industry. 'The pioneering producer' feels

---

16. This quotation is from an interview with Parsons conducted by the authors, as are all other quotes from Parsons unless otherwise indicated.

his work has been stolen, and, for now at least, has had enough.

Parsons trained as a researcher at Britain's London Weekend Television in the 1980s, after two years as a cub reporter on a local daily. He refers to this sojourn in the print media as a formative stage, a professional pre-school that bred a lifelong 'journalistic curiosity' evident in his television work. When he begins to speak of developing '*Survive!*,[17] his description of this curiosity changes from 'journalistic' to 'situationist', a more accurate term; journalists do not, or at least are not supposed to, create the situations they report on. That was where Parsons' talents lay, finding expression in the Channel 4 show *Network 7*, an anarchic assembly of live sketches and irreverent humour. *Network 7* allowed the producers to inflict various demeaning and absurd scenarios on their fall guys. One reporter was locked in a nuclear bunker, and later sent on the road for a fortnight with five pounds to live on. Parsons now can't remember why they were so nasty to the woman in question. 'She's really very nice', he says, looking guilty and a bit confused.

It was a desert island skit on *Network 7* that planted the first seeds of *Survivor*. Five members of the public were dispatched to a remote shore, and filmed in their new lives as castaways, producing footage that Parsons found fascinating. Watching an urbane stockbroker, au fait with

---

17. *Survive!*, as noted in the introduction, is the name of the format commonly produced under the title *Survivor*.

London's better wine lists, transformed into a dirty beach-comber left him with an urge to make further use of the location. Parsons seems to have had an immediate sense of what would later be a cardinal aspect of reality TV's appeal: the impact on 'real people' of unreal situations, in which they're forced to cope with an absence of modern comforts.

Empirical research conducted by Dr Annette Hill, funded by the ESRC, Independent Television Commission and Channel 4, has found that 72 per cent of viewers cite this aspect of reality shows as amongst the most enjoyable. Parsons instinctively appreciated the lure this situationism would hold for the viewer; as befits a man often spoken of as complicit in the dumbing-down of British television, he knew a setting that could make good primetime when he saw it.

Deciding how to use it was to be a lengthy process. Parsons joined 24 Hour Productions, and, along with rock star/impresario/activist Bob Geldof and Waheed Alli, later ennobled by Tony Blair, was instrumental in the merger that established Planet 24, one of the most successful British production companies of the 1990s. It was at 24 that Parsons and his partners won the title 'kings of trash TV', with distinctive productions such as the high-decibel, psychedelic-hued *Big Breakfast*. Despite its use of migraine-inducing presenters, the show was credited with revolutionising morning programming in the UK, though in the process it won Parsons et al. the opprobrium of many critics. This was to become something of a pattern for Planet 24. Their productions rarely failed to hit the target audience, and, crucially for advertisers, it was a younger one than most. Critics railed against the company's output, however, with the flagship *Big Breakfast*, and its trademark mix of celebrity interviews, double entendres and animalistic yowling becoming a symbol of British television's perceived decline. Nevertheless, the ratings spoke for themselves, and by the time Parsons was ready to push *Survive!* in earnest, he was able to get the attention of American TV executives generally uninterested in European wares. Since the arrival of *Survivor*, and later successes of British formats *The Weakest Link* and *Who Wants To Be A Millionaire?* American networks have been noticeably more receptive to ideas from across the water.

Initially, although considerable time and energy were applied to its development, the notion of a desert island game show stalled. There was no defining narrative thrust, and, though Parsons and his team found it easy enough to design a series of mental and physical challenges for their contestants, early versions of the show did not cohere. It was at a meeting in the US that involved, in Parsons' words, 'a lot of pacing up and down in front of whiteboards' that the breakthrough came, with the suggestion that contestants vote each other off the island. This soon became the centrepiece of the format, and by far its most distinctive element, making for an unusually complex game show. *Survivor* contestants, split into two 'tribes' upon arrival, compete for immunity from the elimination votes held at three-day intervals at the 'tribal council' set, a wicker-and-torchlight homage to the temples of primitive tribes as

imagined by B-movie producers. Once a number of contestants have been eliminated (the exact number, and
overall cast size, varying from series to series), the tribes
merge, and the war shifts from factionalism to all-against-
all. With this deceptively simple device, *Survivor* established at its core a progression from the friendly and
clubbable atmosphere of newly arrived contestants, through
ever more Byzantine voting alliances, into utter paranoia
and mistrust in the final episodes. The PR lines 'Trust no
one' and 'There can only be one winner' wrote themselves
once the system was in place, expanding the physically
challenging nature of the environment and competitive
tasks into a layered game that demanded shrewdness and
skilled manipulation. By making the post-merger evictees
into a jury that decides the final winner, the *Survivor* team
ensured there could be payback for all betrayals, requiring
the adoption of complicated play strategies.

Indeed, such was the complexity and ambition of the
format that no one would buy it. ABC and Buena Vista
Television took out an early option, but finally declined to
produce the show, as to do so would have required its
prioritisation above all else. To match the grandeur of the
desert island location (initially the isle of Pulau Tiga in the
South China Sea) it had been decided that the eventual
winner should take a headline-grabbing prize of a million
dollars. Combined with the necessity of roving camera
teams and the building of a production compound with full
editing facilities, this made the series an expensive affair.
Above and beyond the production budget, if the show was

to succeed it would require a massive publicity effort, establishing the uniqueness of *Survivor* in the public mind at recruitment stage and creating a sense of an 'event' when the show was first broadcast. There was no 'natural' audience for an untested formula, and they needed to be marketed into position.

If American networks were wary of making the commitment, their British counterparts were baffled by the whole idea. Parsons took the format to the four networks in the UK, and was met with incomprehension, and a general sense that 'this isn't for us'. He implies that it was simply too grand for commissioning editors in his home country, though, as an independent producer, he holds a certain habitual contempt for such creatures. In one instance, he claims Michael Jackson, later head of Channel 4, asked if he could remove the challenges from the format – which is to say, strip the games from the game show. In the end, the risk was deemed too great by the English-speaking world, and it was the Swedes, with *Expedition Robinson*, who led the way. When the CBS series achieved its landmark audience for the finale one assumes a few executives who'd passed on the format, and with it the opportunity to secure some of the best ratings in history, got busy kicking themselves.

Finalising the *Survivor* format was more than the completion of a game show – it represented the hybridisation of the form, the invention of the 'gamedoc' or 'reality game show', and with it the genesis of an event TV phenomenon that would erupt across the world with unprecedented

speed and force. Parsons' situationist approach was totalising; the complete removal of contestants from their contextualised lives was the first, essential element in the
creation of a self-contained 'pocket world'. For those taking
part, the show became their lives. The 'reality' quotient in
this genre of reality TV is not the 'real', unmediated nature
of the footage, but the establishment of the format's pocket
world as the *sole* reality experienced by contestants through
the duration of filming. Parsons took the fly-on-the-wall
standpoint and inverted traditional debates concerning
'reconstruction' of events in documentary, by constructing
the very walls on which the fly set down. In 2000, British
Big Brother contestants penned an anthem for their incarceration – 'it's only a game show'. Strictly speaking, they
were right – but the game show as evolved into the
gamedoc was not the usual glitzy half-hour showcase of
trivia questions and spinning wheels, split-skirt hostesses
and obnoxious suited hosts. Parsons' innovation, represented in *Survivor*, was to make the game into a complete
universe for its players.

Evidence suggests that viewers comprehend, and
appreciate, this formal aspect of reality TV. As noted above,
Hill's study found that 72 per cent of *Big Brother* viewers
enjoyed 'seeing people live without modern comforts'. The
unreality of the situation, the back-to-basics contours of the
format, proved far more appealing than the opportunity to
indulge voyeuristic appetites, cited by only 35 per cent as a
favourite characteristic of the show. Indeed, the study found
that viewers most enjoyed those elements of the programme

which were intrinsic to the anatomy of *Big Brother*'s pocket world; 68 per cent enjoyed witnessing group conflict, an inevitable aspect of communal living amongst strangers, 65 per cent took pleasure in contestant visits to the diary room. Sixty-one per cent, a little oddly, were quite taken with the spectacle of *Big Brother* contestants attempting the arbitrary and at times distinctly silly tasks set by the producers, while 60 per cent appreciated the docusoap traits of the show – watching people do everyday things. In creating its own context for the weeks and months of contestant behaviour, *Big Brother*, like *Survivor* before it, served up an intriguing morsel to the appetites of social curiosity, a readily comprehensible environment in which social actors are confronted with the unreal constraints of a pocket universe.

The same research has found deep suspicion on the part of viewers towards the 'real' nature of behaviour captured in reality shows and docusoaps. Viewers overwhelmingly believe that people overact for the camera, and part of the appeal of the reality TV experience is waiting for the mask to slip, in moments of stress and conflict, revealing the concealed 'true self' or 'real face' of a contestant. In their hunger for occasions when anger flares and performance gives way to authenticity, we see the audience's fascination with a gaudy, demonstrative selfhood, and a boundless curiosity for the shadowplay of false and real selves. The guarantee of interpersonal conflict created by placing strangers in an unreal pocket world gives free rein to the friction of selves and spontaneity – the perfect showcase for

first-person primacy, with the added novelties of deprivation and bizarre tasks.

Gary Carter, Endemol's international director of licensing and philosopher at large, refers to this aspect of 'reality
entertainment' (as he prefers to call the genre), in speaking
of its appeal: 'in times like these, it's comforting to be able
to turn on the TV, watch the internet, read my phone and
find ten really ordinary folks like me talking about really
ordinary things like those which concern me to people who
sound just like me, and it's not surprising, really, because
they are me'.[18] Described by TV pundit Mariella Frostrup
as 'the Jean-Paul Sartre of light entertainment', Carter
suggests that identification with contestants is an essential
aspect of *Big Brother*'s appeal. The loud first-person inflec-
tion of the genre resonates with an audience conditioned to
value such modes of address – and moreover, in the removal
of selves from social context, the focus is made singular,
unadulterated by the presence of tedious socioeconomic
realities. If one takes Carter's example, the picture of the
modern TV viewer and digital citizen, inundated from all
sides with confused, confusing barrages of information, the
purity of the pocket world as form indeed makes it the
ultimate vehicle of light entertainment. Here there is
no depressing onrush of social meaning – the grim,
serious business of poverty and war, the 'actuality' that
Grierson and his followers sought to educate the masses in,

18. Gary Carter, speaking at a BAFTA seminar, 25 February 2002.

is explicitly excluded by Charlie Parsons' description of reality TV – 'documentary in a controlled environment'. A 'controlled' environment, or, in Carter's phrase, 'constructed scenario', is the antithesis of actuality in the raw. The game shows are their own 'actuality', the creativity in their construction a matter of isolating the first-person presence away from such obstructions as might depress the viewer and interfere with the pornography of the performing self.

These pocket worlds are playgrounds for selves immersed in the retrenched, apolitical apparatus of a selfhood of first-persons; real persons, but in their contrived location so much easier to watch than real selves in the real world. As with the docusoap, the reality game show is not 'about' anything but itself. Charlie Parsons, in creating *Survivor*, served up a world, and, by example, a form, that allows for the top-heavy fixation on the self amongst its kin. The documentary theorist John Corner has argued that we live in 'post-documentary' times; the reality game shows, in their contrivance, are the antithesis of early notions of the documentary. For all that the Griersonians may have failed to address the social meaning of their subjects, the very form of reality game shows blocks out any attempt at its acknowledgement. Documentary in a controlled environment can document nothing but what it controls, the walls of the playground and the totalised consciousness that rises to fill them. What Jon Dovey has called the docusoaps' 'triumph of the trivial' surpasses itself – even trivia, here, is taken away from normal life. The added attractions of exotic locales, purpose-built houses remote from the world and all sources of information about it, exalt the carnival and grant it exclusive attention, as the viewer waits for masks to slip and real persons to show themselves – and, on occasion, their real breasts or pecs. Whatever the prudish responses in focus groups and questionnaires suggest, it seems likely that occasional nudity in *Big Brother* or the shorts-and-bikini heaven of *Temptation Island* (see below), does not exactly hurt their ratings. Perhaps it should not be surprising that the viewers in Hill's study appear, by their own accounts, to be so lacking in voyeurism and prurience.

Charlie Parsons defines reality TV shows as 'producer-created environments that control contestant behaviour', distinguishing the production-side role from the relative passivity of the docusoap-maker. The notion of 'control' here is intriguing. Essentially, the architecture of the format delimits and prescribes the effective range of possible contestant behaviour, belying the claim that as these shows are unscripted, their actions are in an uncomplicated way 'spontaneous'. The format itself is the primary actor in a reality game show; whether the inhospitable regions of *Survivor*, with its institutionalised ostracism and demanding challenges, or the observational 'containment field' of *Big Brother*, with a similar system of exclusion. Contestants may adopt strategies, they may be more or less argumentative, exuberant or promiscuous, but the parameters of free will are circumscribed by the rules that govern and create the situation. Rats can tackle a maze through a number of routes, but there are in the end only so many corridors. Contestants may display their personalities as they choose, but the gameworld, exposing them to a systematic array of pressures, curtails the choices and creates its own desired probabilities. That there is no script does not make for a free-for-all. Far from it. Contestants have in many cases emerged from pocket worlds scathed and confused – the behavioural control function inherent to the formats does not, after all, attempt to elicit their most altruistic, tolerant or humane side. The manufacture of drama requires that pocket worlds include opportunities for pain, for the very trauma and upheaval that first-person primacy adores.

One of the more bizarre – and, in its dubious way, brilliantly effective – formats illustrates the behavioural contortions reality shows inflict on their inhabitants: Fox's *Temptation Island.* If the 'event TV' packaging of reality game shows, establishing in the public mind that a series represents a new and extreme phenomenon, is key to their success, few have understood this so well as the makers of this show. While it's none too difficult to see what draws contestants to *Survivor* or *Big Brother*, given the exposure and possibility of a large cash prize, no one has yet given a credible explanation of why anyone would subject themselves to the absurd pocket universe of *Temptation Island*, which has been cited as an example of reality TV straying into unethical territory by both Charlie Parsons and Anna Brakenhielm, executive producer of the first series of *Expedition Robinson*. *Temptation Island* features no physical extremity in the sense of deprivation, nor a cash prize or winner. The experience invites young, attractive couples to put their relationships 'to the ultimate test', in the form of an array of 'singles', sent to tempt them from monogamy. At the beginning of the series, couples are separated into men's and women's resorts, from which they have no direct contact with their partners. The singles line up before them (in the second American series, this was staged as a baroque pagan ritual reminiscent of the masked ball in Kubrick's *Eyes Wide Shut*). Each partner may prohibit their beloved from dating one single they perceive as a particular threat. Contestants make their first choice of a date from the remaining candidates, and the fun begins in earnest.

Between the rounds of dating, partners are given an occasional video-montage of their other halves cavorting with singles, usually edited to exhibit the most incriminating moments of their behaviour. There is an undeniable, if guilty, fascination with watching the face of a devoted boy- or girl-friend crumple as they see their partner's hands on the body of some unfamiliar third party. Finally, when the show has runs its course, couples are reunited at 'bonfire', an assembly bearing a rather close resemblance to *Survivor*'s tribal council, and confess their sins – or lack thereof – to one another. An American format, *Temptation Island* has not screened sexual encounters between contestants and singles, but their occurrence is baldly inferred, if vaguely described.

The structure of the format allows for a small number of stories to be played out: fidelity and final commitment ('final', at least, insofar as viewers know), infidelity and break-up, infidelity and forgiveness, and various combinations of new relationships emerging with singles. By a clever balancing of the cast at recruitment stage, producers can ensure that there will be an assortment of these outcomes, providing for narratives of true love holding fast, a sprinkling of devilry, and an ambivalent recognition that partners can be imperfect yet finally deserving of forgiveness. By signing their release forms, contestants agree to end up as statistics, each player's feelings and actions manipulated by the production – the walls of the maze forcing them further down the game's paths, leading to infidelity, tears, perhaps heartbreak.

Parsons himself speaks of the reality game show as a hybrid of four forms: the docusoap, game show, drama and talk show. The role played by the first three of these in producing reality TV is self-evident, while the ethos of self-justification embodied in the talk show is present in *Survivor* and many of the reality shows that followed in its wake, in the form of the to-camera explanations of eviction votes seen in *Survivor*'s tribal council and the *Big Brother* diary room. In a prophetic foretaste of criticisms later fired at reality TV, the game show in its earliest incarnations elicited a wounded howl from historian Daniel Boorstin, who attacked the theatricality and contrivance of the form and asked, with touching confusion, 'why are we watching ourselves?' Boorstin's *The Image: A Guide to Pseudo-Events in America*,[19] first published in 1964, now reads as an early, if

---

19. Vintage, 1987 [1964].

partial, comprehension of the narrative direction that would reach its zenith in reality TV, for Boorstin saw the burgeoning momentum of first-person media when they first crept out onto the airwaves.

While Charlie Parsons pushed his format to executives around the world, Dutch company Endemol were increasingly aware of the potential of reality-based shows. The group was formed in 1994 after the merger of the production companies of Joop van den Ende and John de Mol. De Mol had established a track record in the 1980s, producing weekly shows for Dutch TV after a brief stint in radio, while van den Ende's company was a multimedia operation with a profile in TV entertainment and commercial theatre. At the end of that decade, the Dutch TV industry 'went global', with the licensing of programme formats to foreign channels becoming an important source of income. With an eye to the future, de Mol and van den Ende merged their companies on an equal basis, seeking to expand into the European and global markets. By 1996, when the company floated on the Amsterdam stock exchange, its shares oversubscribed by a factor of twenty-five, it had penetrated markets in Portugal, Denmark and Spain, with a strong presence in Germany. The company's stated aim, to become a major global content provider, marks it as a creature of the digital age, committed to multi-platform delivery of 'content', from traditional TV programmes to associated text-message updates. The term 'content provision' is borrowed from the jargon of the web, and represents a changed conception of what operations such as Endemol – no longer classifiable as a 'production company' – can and should do.

There is a certain vacuity to the notion of 'content provision' – filling technological spaces in networks that range from digital television to mobile phones with amorphous units of 'content'. Perhaps the final word on Endemol's nature, and that of its markets, came in the year 2000, when the company was acquired for a reputed 3.5 billion pounds (US\$5,000,000,000) by Telefonica, the largest provider of phone networks in the Spanish and Portugese-speaking worlds. At first glance this seems bizarre, but in the light of *Big Brother*'s multimedia success, represents the first sketchy contours of a new technological order, as the TV industry flirts ever more seriously with the web and mobile phone networks, spanning different delivery platforms to push the same brand. Endemol's *Big Brother* has succeeded in achieving an unprecedented presence across interconnected technologies. Whether, as Endemol claim, this represents a foretaste of a new age, or a grandiose but temporary phenomenon, remains to be seen, but an industry hungry to invest in innovations for the future is inclined to bet on the former, and the company's success with *Big Brother* has won them the admiration and fear of their competitors.

It's difficult to relate the global phenomenon of *Big Brother* to its earliest conception. At a four-hour brainstorming session of the kind John de Mol regularly subjects his top creatives to, an executive made passing reference to the American 'Biosphere Two' experiment, in which a party of scientists were secluded in the sealed environment of a geodesic dome. De Mol is said to have slept little that night, feeling he was on to something big. The idea of putting Biosphere-type seclusion onscreen was a natural extension of trends both on and off TV, with the growing popularity of webcams and surveillance-based reality shows indicating a vast public appetite for observational forms from the banal and pornographic to the simply banal. Elements of the format suggested themselves quickly once the premise was agreed. Originally to be sequestered in *The Golden Cage* (the programme's working title) for a year, inhabitants would be obliged, like the scientists in the original sphere, to grow their own food and maintain complete self-sufficiency. Little of the original blueprint would survive its development, but the vegetable patches and chicken coops of the *Big Brother* house gardens are a tribute to that first meeting.

In 1996, Endemol purchased an option on Charlie Parsons' *Survive!*, along with Strix A.B., who produced the show as *Expedition Robinson*. Endemol, although well known for their ability to sell formats, found it difficult to arouse interest in *Survive!*. At this point Gary Carter, the Planet 24 employee who first contacted Endemol about the format, left his job with Charlie Parsons to become the key player in the Dutch company's international sales efforts, and renewed the option on *Survive!* in May 1997. As the second six-month period neared its end, Carter contacted his former employees at Planet 24 and attempted to renew the option a second time. Parsons refused, feeling that Endemol's failure to secure a production in the twelve months of their license was somewhat odd. He now believes that Endemol were far from serious in their attempts to sell the show, and that Carter, without malicious intent (Parsons takes pains to make it clear that he has nothing against Carter personally, and suspects he 'could have been put in a difficult position at Endemol'), may have been involved in the appropriation of elements of the *Survivor* format for use in the *Golden Cage*, shortly thereafter reborn as *Big Brother.*

The dispute between Parsons and Endemol, at time of writing still dragging through appeals, exploded in 1999 when Parsons first learned of Endemol's *Big Brother* via a fax from CBS, who had seen advance publicity for the first Dutch production. Like *Survive!*, the format featured a voting system by which contestants nominated one another for eviction, although in the case of *Big Brother* the contest was decided by a run-off in which viewers cast the votes. There were, in Parsons' eyes, other areas of similarity that made him immediately suspicious, not least when he learned that there was a striking resemblance between publicity materials used to promote the two shows.

From a Promotional video for *Survive!*, 1997:

> Part entertainment series, part documentary soap, part social experiment, this is *Survive!*

Endemol text on Internet, 1999:

> Part social experiment, part docusoap, part gameshow.

The former, a line of voice-over from the *Survive!* electronic press kit, was narrated by the very Gary Carter who had brokered Endemol's first option deal on the format while at Planet 24, a fact that Parsons takes as evidence of something akin to plagiarism. At the time, he contacted Endemol and demanded the withdrawal of the *Big Brother* format, a request immediately denied, leading him to sue, unsuccessfully, for copyright infringement. Endemol are no strangers to allegations of this kind, and other producers have felt that ideas of theirs have been appropriated by the Dutch company; at a recent BAFTA colloquium on reality TV, when allusion was made to a new American format, Will Macdonald, head of London's Monkey Productions and one of Soho's brightest boys, jokingly asked Gary Carter if the format under discussion was one he'd nicked (stolen) yet. At time of writing, all decisions have gone against the owners of *Survive!*, but Parsons' complaint, though focused on Endemol, relates to the larger architecture of the industry that embraced and expanded upon reality TV. An orgy of imitation was to follow the successes of *Survivor* and *Big Brother*, a cashing-in on the new phenomenon that the 'pioneering producer' sees, somewhat ironically for the man derided as lord supreme of trash TV, as a route to the ongoing degradation of standards and death of innovation in the industry. Parsons may be an odd spokesman for such a vision, but it remains a persuasive one; at its heart, the business of reality TV, riddled with copycatting, has turned on the units that comprise the shows, which is to say, the unit of a globalised TV industry – the format.

The troubled notion of the programme format is almost

as old as television itself, first coming to fruition in the
American game shows of the 1950s. There is no generally
agreed definition of a TV format, and the undefined nature
of the term has become a source of controversy. An organisation exists, in the form of the Format Rights and Pro-
tection Association (FRAPA), committed to 'promote to
producers, broadcasters and the law, the format as a unique
piece of intellectual property'. Although many broadcasters
and production companies have signed up to FRAPA's code
of practice it remains a voluntary charter – in other words,
toothless. A format is a blueprint for a TV show or series,
usually the latter, and can be reduced to the form of a
brochure that enumerates the essential elements of the
show. The question 'what's the difference between a format
and an idea?' is a particularly vexed one, and the legal status
of the format as a unit of intellectual property is vague in
the extreme. Charlie Parsons defines a format as 'a unique
combination of elements that makes the end product sufficiently different to any earlier programme'. Peter Bazalgette, head of Endemol UK, and himself the originator of
some highly successful lifestyle formats, takes the market-
driven line that 'If I can persuade someone in the US or
Australia to buy a licence to produce it as a format, and to
pay me a consultancy fee to advise them on how to make
it, then it is one.'[20] The two men's choice of emphasis –
Parsons on innovation, Bazalgette on international saleability

---

20. The following quotations from Bazalgette are from an interview conducted by
the authors.

– are in very similar ways self-serving. Bazalgette (known as 'Baz', and often referred to by the same critics as both a trash TV 'Prince of Darkness' and a thoroughly nice guy), as a senior figure in Endemol, makes his living through the leasing of, and consultancy on, a wide range of formats; Parsons' career, one of the more notable and controversial for a British independent producer of his generation before *Survivor*, was crowned by the development of the show.

The format may have been around almost as long as television, but as the industry has entered a period of seismic change, so its importance has grown. Bazalgette puts this in simple terms: 'the multichannel age requires a lot more content'. The situation in Britain serves to illustrate this dramatically increased demand. Some twenty years ago, British airwaves hosted three TV channels, BBC1 and 2, and ITV, itself a conglomeration of several companies, each licensed to broadcast at certain times of the week. It was rare indeed for programming in the early 1980s to continue much past midnight – the evening's entertainment ended with the national anthem, and once the last strains of 'God save the Queen' gave way to silence, the screen filled up with night-time snow and static. Within a few years, a new network was launched, and the broadcast schedule began a slow expansion of its hours, until at last the airwaves flashed with moving colour through the night.

Twenty years on, it's all but meaningless to conduct a count of channels available in the UK. With competing packages on offer via satellite, cable, and the digital spectrum, many viewers have access to dozens of channels, many of which attract audiences too small to register on the ratings system. This has led to widespread fear and trembling among network executives at the prospect of audience fragmentation. There is an element of smoke and mirrors to this, as the digital and satellite revolutions have so far reached only a minority of European households, while in the US it is widely agreed that the networks have had a soft landing, and the potential for fragmentation has yet to be realised. But the expectation that audiences will shrink and Balkanise, and a continuing decline of overall audience size, has led to a panic unsupported by the actual extent of change in viewing patterns. In the words of Charlie Parsons: 'no one knows what the fuck is going on with TV'. As such, a format or programme that has the capacity to win a large viewership across international boundaries has become the Holy Grail. As Bazalgette puts it, if 'an idea of proven value can be turned into local content' (e.g. an Endemol format), produced in national variations across the world, channel-side hunger for it will be insatiable.

The implications of this congeal around the prospect of an increased homogeneity of programming across the world. As television becomes a far more competitive business, the ever greater nervousness of TV executives worldwide has resulted in a situation where 'as soon as something is seen to work, like *Big Brother*, other countries and other channels have to get the idea, or a lookalike right away. When something works the locusts arrive, they rip it off, they update it, it spreads like wildfire' (Bazalgette). Countering the charge that the locusts thus ensure that television everywhere will eventually look the same, Bazalgette points out that this is the reality of globalisation in many areas, citing as examples the spread of the English, Spanish and Chinese languages and the growth of multi-national brands across industries. In an implicit rebuke to Parsons, he admits that 'there may be a few rip-offs at the fringes of the business' – he does not specify examples – 'but people are doing very well out of them [the formats]'. He does not need to point out that Parsons is one of these people; he and his partners at Planet 24 netted a cool five million apiece on selling the company to Carlton, but Parsons retained the leasing rights to *Survivor* via the company Castaway. It continues to outperform all other reality shows in the US, and Parsons has the grace to admit that his grievance 'doesn't matter all that much'. While he feels that others have profited from his work without giving him proper credit, he himself will not go hungry.

Parsons maintains that it was the spectacle of the locusts descending on the carcass of *Survive!* that led him to sue Bazalgette's employers at Endemol Netherlands, to establish in law whether the format could indeed enjoy recognition as a unique piece of intellectual property. Besides the principle, however, there is a distinctly private aspect to his grievance; he has seen the other reality shows based on the conceit of stranding contestants in remote and inhospitable locations,[21] as more or less direct rip-offs of *Survivor*, whose

---

21. i.e. *Shipwrecked*, *Castaway*, and, above all, *I'm A Celebrity ... Get Me Out Of Here!*, discussed in the postscript to this chapter, below.

relative failure on British television is a matter of deep disappointment to him. Network bafflement at the *Survive!* format in the UK led to its being screened after *Big Brother* had already given reality game shows their British debut, and, as a result, he has felt wounded that British viewers are wont to see *Big Brother* as the 'original' show. It is undeniable that the spread of reality TV has indeed had much to do with the two shows 'entering the water', in practice handing over to competitors the 'essential elements' that made for their success. 'The water', a notional expanse of cultural space referred to by producers, is simply 'the world' – once something is onscreen, imitation is inevitable.

Reality shows proliferated at an astonishing rate in the aftermath of 1999–2000's *Survivor* and *Big Brother* triumphs. An example from each side of the pond demonstrates how the essential elements of each could be lifted and removed to a new setting, juxtaposed around the conceit of a new pocket world to produce a show that sought to cash in on the reality craze with little by way of structural originality. *Love Cruise*, an American format screened by the Fox network in 2001, took the all-important element of the contestant-eviction voting system and transferred it, along with a final jury of ex-contestants strikingly similar to *Survivor*'s 'tribal council', to the setting of a cruise ship, where contestants were paired off with members of the opposite sex, apparently in the hope of romances blooming. The highly personalised nature of the game made for extravagant bitchiness and double-dealing on all sides, with the action of the show consisting of the emergence and dissolution of voting alliances guaranteed to maximise conflict and strife amongst contestants. It was the social dynamic of *Survivor*, without the visual scope of the island location or allegedly 'life-enhancing' aspects of the long struggle with the environment. As such, *Love Cruise* is little more than a distillation of the darker aspects of *Survivor*'s narrative.

In the UK, the interactive element of *Big Brother* was imported into the leafy glades of *Eden*, a format of inter-activity gone wild. Where *Big Brother* won the loyalty of its most ardent fans by granting them control over the eventual outcome, *Eden* empowered viewers not only to decide the eventual winner of the game in a public vote, but to select the contestants from a range of vetted applicants, and even to elect the 'leader' of the group each week. Viewers also selected what contestants ate, what special delivery packages they'd get and so forth – thus interactivity was extended in every corner of their sojourn. The show ran in an early evening slot used by Channel 4 to cater to its young viewership with an array of teen- and young-adult-targeted programmes, in an attempt to take advantage of this demographic's presumed appetite for interactivity. As with the example of *Love Cruise* and *Survivor*, it is unlikely that *Eden* would have developed had the locusts not had *Big Brother* to descend upon.

As Bazalgette intimates, both Endemol and Parsons have done well from their formats. There is an important dif-ference. Parsons, a TV man through and through, can sound like one of his own critics when he bemoans the spectacle of the contemporary TV industry, invoking a glorious past in which Britain's TV output was 'this country's Hollywood'. Endemol, by contrast, have shifted their rhetoric and aspects of their practice away from an exclusive focus on television as a medium – the future of reality entertainment, as Endemol see it, lies in a dazzling array of networks, online and off. The lasting impact of the reality game shows may lie in the trail Endemol have blazed, creating the first commercially successful multimedia event. If one were to take their rhetoric seriously, *Big Brother* is but the herald of far-reaching revolution.

Whatever the truth of its development process, *Big Brother*, with humble beginnings as the non-voting, challenge-free *Golden Cage*, had by 2002 achieved a unique success, of quite a different order than *Survivor*'s. In two separate but related areas, the show pioneered a range of new technologies, both in the production itself and in its dissemination across interconnected platforms. *Big Brother* houses are online around the clock, with many countries featuring virtually[22] live streams on cable channels such as Britain's E4, that allow the truly obsessive, and perhaps the drug-addled, to watch contestants sleep in real time. The unveiling of a new *Big Brother* house is an event in itself, with garishly stylish design and ever greater camera counts (thirty-three mounted in *Big Brother 3 UK*). With text message updates available via SMS, and voting options from

---

22. 'Virtually' owing to a fifteen-minute time lag necessary to prevent the airing of foul language during daytime and early evening viewing.

simple phone lines to digital remote controls, *Big Brother* provided more opportunities for viewer interaction than any earlier show.

The economic significance of *Big Brother* as a multimedia enterprise is by far its most imposing aspect. With the launch of *Big Brother 3*, the British version of the format achieved a masterful cross-platform brand saturation that saw the series garner record ratings – and, perhaps more importantly, a record number of eviction votes. This was achieved in the face of a hostile press, with tabloids declaring themselves '*Big Brother*-free zones'. Despite a striking absence of the kind of headline feeding frenzy that developed around the show in its first two years, *Big Brother 3* was an immediate ratings success, outperforming its 2001 predecessor from the first episode. Overall, 22.5 million votes were cast in the weekly polls, with a vast number submitted, quite profitably, via SMS. Channel 4 had undertaken a novel kind of sponsorship deal with mobile phone network O2, and the results underlined the potential of multi-platform delivery. The live streams broadcast on the *Big Brother* website were no longer free-to-view; two weeks into the series, a ten pound fee was levied for those subscribing to the cameras. There was an initial flurry of protest from web purists, to whom payment for content is anathema, but the internet has come a long way from its early idealism, and before long, over 25,000 viewers had signed up.

O2 held an enviable position, with their logo and advertisements before the eyes of millions of fans as each

episode began. As their sponsorship deal involved the provision of mobile phone services to the production, the
company was emblazoned across every platform that held up
Big Brother; the terrestrial bulletins functioned as a gateway,
nudging viewers towards a plethora of *Big Brother*/O2/
Channel 4 services, on cable channel E4 (which received its
best ever ratings with the magazine show *Big Brother's Little
Brother*, a viewing experience not unlike being trapped in an
elevator with two hysterical boy bands and an angry dog),
the web, digital interactive services and mobile phones. Past
studies had shown that interactive sponsorship arrangements achieve far higher rates of brand recall than linear
sponsorhip deals restricted to one medium, with an interactive cereal advert attaining 2.4 times more brand recall
than a straightforward commercial in 1996. As such, O2's
embrace of the Endemol brand was inspired – it assured
them a ubiquity and audience as wide and deep as *Big
Brother*'s own. The O2 brand was not so much pushed by the
programme as a part of it, a constant background that
naturally, and almost unobtrusively, burned its way into the
minds of viewers. With money rolling in from the digital,
online and mobile phone platforms, the production shrug-
ged off the most serious advertising downturn in recent TV
history, and turned a seven-figure profit for a struggling
Channel 4. The network's average price for a thirty-second
advertising spot was £18,000 in 2002. *Big Brother*, a valuable property from the start, boosted the going rate to
£30,000 in its early weeks. In the course of the series, it
more than doubled.

The decision to charge for access to the live streams was justified by Peter Grimsdale, head of cross-platform development at Channel 4, with reference to the show's success. Streaming becomes a more expensive prospect as more surfers sign on, and with Channel 4 facing a difficult year, 'free streaming was simply not an option'. Where in the past a proportion of the revenue from viewers' votes had gone to charity, 2002 saw it split amongst Channel 4, Endemol and O2, a mercantilism that saw each enriched by millions. The research conducted by Annette Hill, cited above, purported to find a general indifference towards interactivity on the part of viewers. In her words, 'it's too early'. However, when a multi-platform assault on the senses is as sophisticated and far-reaching as that of *Big Brother 3*, it may well be that viewers, semi-conscious of the presence of the O2 logo in the corner of the screen as they log on to an interactive quiz, are simply unaware of the impact of what they view. Certainly, it seems that the cross-platform dimensions of the series allowed it to shrug off a uniformly derisory press. As with the advance reaction to an audience fragmentation not yet fully realised, it is the potential of the interactive platforms rather than their take-up to date that influences the industry – and the two issues are not unconnected. By straddling media from mobile phones to radio, the web and analogue TV, *Big Brother* is far more resistant to fragmentation than conventional programming. There are few communication technologies in public use which are unable to access *Big Brother*-related information, and wherever you may land in the fragmented territory of the superhighway, there will be a *Big Brother* node to hook up to.

Gary Carter has proposed *Big Brother* as the first step towards a future in which 'the broadcaster is not the brand, and the programme is not the brand, but audiences are branded communities who experience a single event in many different ways, synchronously and asynchronously'.[23] Perhaps unsurprisingly, given the speed at which *Big Brother* spread across the world, 'branding' is an important concept to Endemol, and Carter, their resident seer, makes much of it. Not only are audiences to be branded as communities, but the self, he informs us, has always been a brand, part of 'a constructed reality separate from the body'. The white heat of technology gives off intoxicating fumes, and such rhetorical flights of fancy show a certain delirium. That the 'self is a construct' may be uncontroversial, but the sleight of hand by which 'construct' and 'brand' become synonymous is a rather striking piece of gibberish. Much of this rhetoric is culled from the already quaint propaganda of online one-worlders, who a few years ago predicted the wholesale replacement of terrestrial reality by the worldwide web. Many of them are now looking for jobs.

The choice of rhetoric is nevertheless revealing when one considers that Endemol have globalised on the back of the programme's success, establishing a stateside operation which has fared comparatively badly with America's *Big*

---

23. The quotations from Carter in this section are from his speech at the BAFTA seminar, 25 February 2002.

Brother, but rather well with 'extreme stunt' game show *Fear Factor* and a host of other projects; their marketing clearly works. Endemol's frank view of their audience as 'brandable' suggests an elevation of marketing to the rank of primary social agent, and at times it sounds as though a tacit contempt laces their conception of the viewership. When John de Mol says that 'young people these days care about nothing but fun, excitement, and what's in it for me',[24] he may seem approving, or at least indulgent. Spoken in the right voice, or perhaps just listened to correctly, the same words are a brutal dismissal of millions of people, decried as narrowly self-interested cretins. Those who deal in virtuality at times lose sight of flesh and blood. Carter refers to the attacks of 11 September as a 'PR event', a 'symbolic and on-message' campaign. 'This was the entertainment age in search of spectacle, and we dutifully played our part with every technology at our command.' Arresting as footage of the twin towers being struck by jets was at the time, this 'PR campaign' was above and beyond all else a massacre. To conceive of it primarily as 'visually impressive' is obscene.

While words delivered by Endemol about their viewers can sound harsh, John de Mol does not appear to deliver them in such a light – although Carter begins and ends his set piece with an ambiguous intonation of the words 'Thank you so much for coming. You really do make all the difference.' Cloaked in references to post-modernity and its

---

24. *Newsweek*, 10 July 2000.

'entropy of irony', it is both impossible and irrelevant to know whether Carter's oratory is – or aspires to being – serious. But the company's stated aim to 'change the very nature of creativity' via interactive media, and its embrace of the outer reaches of a vocabulary that fetishises technology, comprise a bold manifesto: the complete transformation of mind and self into market-hungry units of consumption. Carter envisages a future where entertainment media will be far more than posts receiving signals:

> I'm waiting for media which can convey the complexity of unpredictable information ... waiting for media which are truly interactive and understand presence, can communicate with your presence, which can suggest with which shows you might want to interact ... which can surround you as you enter it ... what exactly will be reality then? ... I'm dreaming of the moment we all become part of one network.

In reality, the rhetoric of revolutionary change at the hands of technology invariably outpaces the facts on the ground, and the multimedia penetration that *Big Brother* has achieved may prove to be less the herald of a new age than a lucky stroke of marketing. Nevertheless, by virtue of their market position, Endemol will in practice define by example the intellectual property units that interactive content comprise, and the first entertainment products on new generation mobile phones are likely to come from them. The vision may be self-aggrandising and ahistorical, but it is one we are condemned to hear more of.

The success of *Big Brother* led Endemol to rebrand itself,

dropping the 'entertainment' from its title to become simply 'Endemol'. A new logo was adopted, resembling a blob of dough that's been used as an ashtray, but apparently representing 'both an eye and a world observed'. This presumably means something, though in a manner, like all things beneath the sky of the post-modern Gods that Carter's rhetoric pays homage to, either 'ironic, iconic, or camp'. Perhaps, like *Big Brother* itself, 'the symbolic eye and world observed' is all three, staring back and forth from and to its interactive future.

Postscript: I'm A Celebrity, See You in Court . . .

At the age of thirty-seven, Natalka Znak's career, impressive from the start, was lent the kind of sudden visibility achieved only by producers whose work has set the media on fire (and, in this case, won audience shares of up to 43 per cent). The executive producer of the British version of *Temptation Island*, and originator of vacation-resort based docusoaps such as *Ibiza Uncovered*, notorious for their showcasing of the British abroad, in states of near undress and pronounced drunkenness, Znak was already seen as an up and coming star. The 'uncovered' formula was successful, leading to a series of similar shows on Sky One and Channel 4. *Temptation Island*, once on-screen, created little stir in the UK, beyond the initial moral outcry, but did nothing to damage Znak's reputation, earning her the respect of executives at Fox. If Znak was remotely troubled by the criticisms levelled at a format that invites contestants to play with their lives, she kept it to herself.

It was as LWT's head of reality TV that Znak was to rise to international prominence, becoming one of the hottest properties in broadcasting. In conjunction with a high-profile development unit, The Hothouse, established to bring the creativity and risk-taking of an independent production company to the ITV network, Znak came up with a format – instantly described by virtually every commentator as *'Celebrity Survivor'*[25] – that was to become a national talking point in Britain for the few weeks of its run. The *Survivor* references in every article on the subject were not lost on Messrs Parsons and Geldof; within weeks of the show airing to rapturous applause, the boys of Planet 24, via the *Survivor*-owning company Castaway, were heading back to court.

While the *Big Brother* lawsuit was based upon what can seem, to casual viewers, an arcane claim of similarities existing between elements of the gameworlds, the resemblance between *I'm A Celebrity ... Get Me Out Of Here!* and *Survivor* could not be more straightforward. Znak's show took eight 'minor celebrities' and stranded them in the Australian rainforest. Amongst the cast were 'psychic' Uri Geller and Tara Palmer-Tomkinson, a gossip columnist and vocal rehab graduate who became symbolic of the 'It girl'

---

25. A sample of headlines from the BBC: 'Viewers warm to star Survivor' (BBC Online, 27 August 2002); 'Celebrity "Survivor" in the pipeline' (11 July 2002); 'Celebrity Survivor splits audience' (8 September 2002); 'DJ Tony wins celebrity Survivor' (8 September 2002).

phenomenon – young, attractive women with a great deal
of money who attend parties as a way of life and all too
often write about it. Other featured superstars included a
disc jockey past his prime, the wife of a disgraced former
Conservative politician, and a model who boxes. These
notables lived at the whim of the voting/viewing audience,
composed in part of a surprising number of broadsheet
luminaries, such as novelist and commentator supreme
Mark Lawson, who confessed themselves addicted to the
show. The central action of the programme took the form of
public eviction votes and 'bush tucker trials', in which
contestants were forced to eat unpleasant dishes, much like
a number of *Survivor* and *Fear Factor* challenges, and to
survive on a daily allocation of rations. The location, and
the manner of its filming, were barely distinguishable from
any series of *Survivor.*

Critics noted all of this, with the UK's *Guardian*
remarking that *I'm A Celebrity . . .* had been perceived as 'the
most derivative format going – a mix of *Survivor*, *Celebrity
Big Brother* and Sky One's *Fear Factor*'.[26] Znak's response to
this comment embodies the attitudes Parsons has objected
to in the industry at large: 'I don't see that as a criticism. I
see that as common sense. You have to see what works well.
Isn't that the job of everyone developing programmes, to
take from other programmes? Pop Stars becomes Pop Idol.
It is how you put the elements together that counts.'[27]

---

26. *Guardian*, 9 September 2002.
27. Ibid.

Many in the industry might agree. Parsons and Geldof responded as follows;

> It is with regret that the owners of Castaway Television Productions Ltd, Waheed Alli, Bob Geldof and Charlie Parsons have issued legal proceedings today against Granada and London Weekend Television for damages and an injunction for infringement of copyright and passing off.
>
> 'I'm a Celebrity ... Get Me Out Of Here!' was not made by or with the consent of Castaway, the owner of the worldwide rights in the international hit television series 'Survivor', contrary to widespread belief.
>
> Survivor took years to develop in a process costing hundreds of thousands of pounds. Castaway regards the protection of its intellectual property rights most seriously.[28]

As, indeed, does CBS, whose executives responded to news of a possible American version of the show with a demand that ABC and Granada abandon their discussions, and pledge in writing that 'they will not broadcast or license in the United States any programming based in whole or part on the Celebrity series'. ABC were cagey as to how they would respond, and at time of writing it remains unclear whether the networks will meet in court. Parsons and Geldof, the latter seeming to have been designated as the public face of the suit, continue to insist that they are fighting for a principle, while LWT's response – disavowing any connection between the shows – was predictable enough. Those familiar with the first Castaway suit have

---

28. Castaway press release, issued 26 September 2002, signed Charlie Parsons.

murmured that, like its predecessor, the challenge over *I'm A Celebrity* is unlikely to succeed, but rumours of a coming change in format law are beginning to circulate.

Znak put the success of '*Celebrity Survivor*' down to casting, which, she says, is everything in reality TV. Or perhaps, the true message of the past few years is that the success of a reality TV show depends on how well it 'combines elements' from past productions, and that there truly is no bottom to the barrel that these formats fill. '*Celebrity Survivor*', in its mix of plaintive casualties from the outer reaches of the media, willing to face mockery in return for attention, games and locations seen in other shows, and an overall ethos of glorying in its own absurdity, is the zenith of atrocious, derivative television. In all probability, though, Natalka Znak's just getting started, and appears, every bit as much as Endemol, to be very much a creature of her times.

4

STANFORD [29]

On the 9 August 1971, officers of the Palo Alto Police Department swept into the homes of nine young men, arresting them on charges of armed robbery and burglary. They led the suspects from their homes, searched them spreadeagled against squad cars, and informed them of the charges. They charged the nine at the central Palo Alto lock-up, subjected them to a more thorough strip search, then dumped them, chained and blindfolded, in holding cells. Some hours later, the police moved them to jail, where they signed them over to the care of Stanford County Prison correctional officers.

Even by the standards of Governor Reagan's California, conditions in the Stanford County jail were harsh. Small three-man cells housed the inmates, who were issued with a uniform of nylon head-cap, rubber sandals and a loose dress-like smock, to be worn without underwear, and each given

---

29. This chapter is based on the account of the Stanford Prison Experiment given on Philip Zimbardo's website, <www.prisonexp.org>

an identifying number. The first night of their incarceration, they were woken at 2.30 a.m. for a numerical roll-call. The guards, new to their jobs, had some difficulty establishing control over their charges, who laughed as they stumbled over their new code numbers. The guards were not amused, and ordered the prisoners to continue calling out their numbers until they could do so in perfect sequence. Prisoner 819, having laughed out loud, was spontaneously ordered to do twenty-three press-ups. The prison governor, overseeing the activity, thought this punishment inappropriate for a prison setting, but some time later he learned that German concentration camp guards had favoured the same tactic. The prisoners abruptly stopped laughing, and obeyed.

On the second day, the prisoners rebelled. They barricaded themselves inside their cells and hurled insults at their jailors. The guards conferred, uncertain how to handle such a volatile situation. None had worked in the penal system before, and found themselves confronted by a prison officer's worst-case scenario: insurrection. They called in three officers on leave, and rushed the cells with fire extinguishers, blasting inmates off the barricades with streams of CO_2. Before long, the prison was theirs again, and they stripped the nine men naked, incarcerating the ringleaders in solitary confinement. Those inmates deemed to have been least involved with the rebellion were given back their uniforms and taken to a 'privilege cell', where they were fed, in sight of the most unruly agitators, whose rations were withheld as punishment. In a classic exercise of arbitrary power, an hour later the guards summarily switched the prisoners in the privilege cells with three rebels, leading to speculation amongst inmates as to which of their fellow sufferers were the informers. While the prisoners viewed each other with suspicion, their nascent unity destroyed, the guards, aware now of the common threat they faced, began to cohere as a unit.

None of the officers had been prepared for the sense of danger they now felt. They knew, after all, that the charges against the young men were false, and had not expected such insurgency amongst their clean-cut, middle-class prisoners, for the two groups – guards and inmates – were engaged in an elaborate role play. They were all volunteers, recruited by social psychologist Philip Zimbardo to take part in a two-week experiment. It was a time when social psychology had taken on a distinctly situationist character, with leading researchers producing experimental scenarios similar to the reality shows that would emerge some twenty years later; the Stanford County Prison Experiment easily passes the Charlie Parsons test – an environment was contrived to elicit, record and interpret responses. This was no more 'formal' an experiment, in terms of its design, than the 'experimental ethos' of *Expedition Robinson*. Zimbardo, like Parsons, went in with no hypothesis, and no quantitative measures could be applied to his results. Like Parson's scenarios, it was an experiment in the purest and least scientific sense, a *what if?* posed in the construction of an artificial, totalising world. Zimbardo's methods, too, were not that far from the privation tests of *Survivor*; what happens, he'd asked himself, to good people in bad places?

The 'good kids' of the experiment were recruited through the local press, and subjected to a reality TV-type screening process – a battery of personality tests and psychiatric interviews, background and health checks. The final sample of twenty-four were divided at random into inmate and guard groups. All were college students, with clean records and no history of violence. Several of those allocated to the 'guard' group were staunch opponents of the war in Vietnam. The products of America's post-war boom, the volunteers' lives were situated far from the fast track to prison of the urban poor; the conveyor belt of poverty, drugs, unemployment and petty crime was all but unknown to them. Nothing in their experience prepared them to do more than play-act the roles of guards and prisoners, construing each role in the light of the movies and TV shows they'd grown up with.

Almost immediately, the atmosphere of play-acting turned into something more sinister. The prison was designed to maximise their sense of remove from the outside world – the cells were without windows or clocks, and the central corridor was blocked at both ends. In the aftermath of the rebellion, the consciousness of guards and prisoners underwent dramatic change. The guards' regime grew ever more hard-line and unendurable. From the moment the rebellion began, the guards had treated the prisoners as though they posed a real threat to their authority, each side growing into, and becoming, their given roles. As the guards smashed their way through barricades, grabbing and forcibly subduing prisoners, one inmate screamed out 'Simulation! It's a fucking simulation.' If this would have gone without saying at one point, it was now a plaintive call, and no longer sounded credible.

The period after the rebellion saw the guards grow more brutal, and the stress this placed on inmates began to appear dangerous; after thirty-six hours, one prisoner lapsed into a state of high trauma, and had to be released. Inmate 8612 presented textbook symptoms of incipient nervous collapse, crying uncontrollably, with intermittent fits of rage and disorganised cognition. Zimbardo later noted that his own 'role' as prison superintendent had come, by this point, to dominate his consciousness; presented with an experimental subject in the throes of nervous breakdown, he saw rather a canny prisoner on the make, faking his symptoms to get out of jail. While pleading with the guards, 8612 made repeated requests for access to a lawyer, though he had committed no crime and was, in theory, free to leave. All of the volunteers could at any time cry 'stop', 'I quit', but in the course of six days, none of them did so. Zimbardo would later write that they had lost the capacity to conceive of this option – trapped in the defenceless mindset of the inmate, the young men simply could not assert their prerogative and walk.

After 8612's release, a rumour spread through the ranks of guards that the disturbed young man had been faking, and was planning to return with reinforcements to liberate the remaining captives. Zimbardo placed an informer in with 8612's former cellmates, and then visited his liaison at the Palo Alto Police Department, who had lent officers to the experiment for the dramatic mass arrest. Zimbardo explained that his 'prisoners' were on the verge of an escape attempt, and asked for the use of real jail cells, so they could be removed from the experimental prison before their 'liberators' arrived. The police declined his request, and a furious Zimbardo returned to Stanford County jail, preparing to dismantle it and herd his inmates, blindfolded and chained, into a storeroom, while he waited for the 'cavalry's' arrival. The rescue attempt never materialised. It had been a jailhouse rumour.

Made to look foolish, the guards' malevolence increased. Prisoners were ordered to clean toilets with their bare hands, and the tedious roll-call number counts became more frequent and repetitive. Visiting hours saw the families of inmates accept the strictures placed on their loved ones; they were subjected to classic institutional harassment – registration procedures and unnecessary waiting periods – before they were allowed to spend ten minutes with their brother, son or boyfriend in the presence of a guard. When they saw the conditions in which their sons were held some of the parents became concerned. While heard to complain amongst themselves, they were meekness personified in their dealings with Zimbardo, who would later write, in reference to his conversation with a visiting mother, 'She was reacting to the authority I was subconsciously becoming – as superintendent of the Stanford County Jail.'

Zimbardo's own behaviour in the course of the experiment was indicative of just how powerful the contrivance could be; the Stanford Prison setting cast its spell on all involved, including the scientist whose blueprint was enacted there. While the prisoners and guards fell into character with a verisimilitude few actors could match, Zimbardo appeared to undergo his own transformation, into a less than liberal prison warden. His scientific objectivity, and methodology, were displaced by the concerns of a warden with a population to control; when the rumour of an imminent escape attempt began to circulate, the responses appropriate to his role as experimenter – monitoring the speed of rumour transmission and its behavioural consequences – were passed over in favour of an attempt to ensure the security of 'his prison'. Zimbardo on three occasions involved third parties, all authority figures – the Palo Alto Police, the chaplain, and finally a lawyer – and implies in his write-up that the simulated nature of the spectacle was withheld from them. Even if these outside collaborators were informed, however, their 'real status' further confused the prisoners. A chaplain came to visit, and asked the inmates how they expected to secure their releases. Did they not realise that their only hope was to engage a lawyer? Several of the inmates, who to this point had remained aware that their experience was just a simulation, were frightened and bewildered once the priest had left; confronted with a real member of the clergy, they no longer knew where the lines were drawn. Was the priest real? The prison? The charges against them?

Zimbardo's own confusion became clear when a second prisoner, 819, began to show signs of severe distress. Refusing to visit the chaplain, he was cajoled out of his cell, only to collapse in floods of tears. Zimbardo removed his chains and cap, and sent him to recuperate. The guards, meanwhile, lined up his fellow inmates, and led them in a chant of 'Prisoner 819 damaged, defaced, and tampered with prison property. Prisoner 819 did a bad thing. Prisoner 819 did a bad thing. Prisoner 819 did a bad thing.'

Zimbardo later wrote:

> As soon as I realised 819 was hearing all this, I raced into the room where I had left him, and what I found was a boy crying hysterically, while in the background his fellow prisoners were yelling and chanting that he was a bad prisoner, that they were being punished because of him. No longer was this a chant or count, disorganised and full of fun, as we saw on the first day. It was marked by its conformity, by its compliance, by its absolute unison. It was as if a single voice was saying '819 is bad'. Or like a million Hitler Jugend chanting 'Heil Hitler' in a torchlight rally.

Zimbardo's notes suggest that it was at this point he realised the situation was out of control. 'Let's leave', he said to 819, who tearfully refused, wanting to return to his cell and prove that no, he was a *good* prisoner ...

> At that point I said, 'Listen, you are not 819. My name is Doctor Zimbardo. I am a psychologist, and this is not a prison. This is just an experiment, and those are students, just like you. Let's go.' He stopped crying suddenly and looked up at me just like a small child awakened from a

nightmare and said 'Okay, let's go.' It's also clear that what I was doing was convincing myself of the statement I had just made.

Although Zimbardo found it necessary to convince himself that he truly was a psychologist, rather than a warden, and had already witnessed three subjects suffer hysterical breakdowns in the course of the study, he did not yet see fit to abort. In the days that followed, further blurring of real/ simulated took place; the chaplain, having recommended to the subjects' visitors that they contact a lawyer, succeeded in bringing legal counsel to the jail. Parole hearings were held, and the prisoners were asked if they would relinquish their participation fees in exchange for release. All but two consented. When instructed to return to their cells and await a verdict, the prisoners complied like sheep, even though, by referring to their payment for participation, Zimbardo had underlined that they were just volunteers, and free to leave. None of them appeared to understand this anymore.

On day six of an intended two-week run, Zimbardo aborted the experiment. The inmates were evincing signs of concentration camp or gulag inmate behaviour – turning on any of their number who the guards singled out as 'bad', showing decreasing levels of concern for one another when the authorities stirred up division, and in many cases exhibiting the hysterics and generalised collapse often deployed as an escape mechanism in event of unbearable stress. Whatever the 'simulated' status of the experiment, the suffering of prisoners was real enough – as was the social withdrawal and unresponsiveness, observed on the part of each inmate, as though the prison air was rife with viral spores of schizophrenia. The guards, meanwhile, showed signs of enjoying their power, and capitulated to the wild joy of sadism – there were those who seemed upset by the behaviour of their fellow guards, and did not engage in abuse of prisoners; but, crucially, they did nothing to stop those guards who did. In Zimbardo's words, no doubt a description of many real-world prison orders, 'it was the good guards who helped maintain the prison, although the bad guards set the tone'.

In true early 1970s fashion, an encounter group was held once the experiment had been aborted, with guards, staff and prisoners invited to express their feelings, and attempt to draw what personal lessons they could from the affair. Many spoke of how the Stanford Prison Experiment had lost its simulated character early on. In the words of Prisoner 416: 'I forgot my reasons for being there ... I really had no life of my own except what happened to me in that small white room ... I began to feel that that identity, that the person that I was, that had decided to go to prison, was distant from me, was remote, until finally, I wasn't that, I was ... I was 416. I was really my number.'

5

THE SHRINKS

During the court case in Holland, Endemol's defence stated that part of the development of *Big Brother* involved research into 'comparable experiments', citing the Stanford Prison Experiment as one example. If not a consciously direct influence, the study shares much with other reality game shows. Charlie Parsons talks about how *Survivor* is a situationist idea, and Stanford was among the most situationist of experiments. He admits that producers exercise a 'terrible power' over contestants, and the puppet master role of producers of reality television is analogous to the figure of the social psychologist, omniscient within the frame of his created world. It is a seductive position to be in, and nurtures a sense of aesthetic flamboyance. Zimbardo (like Stanley Milgram, of the equally notorious 'obedience to authority' experiments) is sometimes spoken of as being a frustrated artist, and reality TV creatives can equally be viewed as industry versions of today's conceptual artists, creating templates for installation-worlds.

In 2001, just as interest in the Stanford Experiment and

social psychology at large were enjoying a renewed surge of interest, Zimbardo was elected to be president of the American Psychological Association (APA) for the following year. He puts the revival down in part to the rise of reality television, and himself sees the study as a forerunner of the genre: 'The reason why the Stanford Prison study has legs after thirty years ... reality TV is making it popular, people are discovering this is an interesting genre.'

The relationship between psychology and reality television is more than one of parent to runaway child, though. Psychologists are involved in all the major shows, in the screening processes, as monitors during filming, and at times as advisors to the contestants, often also providing 'aftercare' once the series have finished. The productions put great store by the efficacy of the screening processes, a mixture of interviews, pep talks and personality tests. These provide the shows with a robust defence against charges of exploitation, and give the appearance that a production's concern for its participants' welfare is more than glancing. They also provide the production with information that helps achieve a combustive and varied mix of personalities.

One contestant told us about his screening interview with Brett Kahr, consultant psychotherapist on the British *Big Brother* series. The prospective contestant was asked if he saw any parallels between his desire to enter the house and the divorce of his parents, given that one of his children was now the same age as he had been when his own father absconded from the family unit. The interview resembled a therapy session – a psychologist asks you about your family history, your motivations, fears and so forth – but it was not subject to therapeutic confidentiality, and the contestant knew the information he provided would form the basis of an assessment of his suitability for the show. It was thus double-edged, both a session with a psychotherapist and an audition. Josh Rafter, from the same series, put it this way in an *Observer* interview,[30] here talking about the availability of consultation once inside the house: 'You're told that you can talk to a psychiatrist in the diary room of the Big Brother house. But you always worry about talking to them frankly.' There have been rumours that during the first American series a psychologist advised a contestant they were at risk of psychological harm, though this hasn't been substantiated. In any case, the value of the psychological help on offer must be questionable, as the psychologist, with no straightforward duty of care, plays a double role, both assessor and protector. Contestants slip between terms in how they describe the consultants; at times they are variously 'psychotherapists', 'psychiatrists', 'psychologists'. The confusion of distinction reflects that found in the larger population, but may also be borne of the fact that these figures are at times all of these, and also none. Primarily, they're production-side consultants, mind crew.

In *Big Brother UK* there was a second psychologist on hand, Peter Collett, to offer interpretations of contestant behaviour on air. These tended to be bland readings of body

---

30. 'Big Brother sucks you up and spits you out, warns Josh', *Observer*, 27 January 2002.

language, linguistic mannerisms and the like, complementing the trashier or more salacious moments the series provided with occasional 'insights' into the house dynamic, lending the show an air of pseudo-scientific legitimacy, and harking back to the early influences Endemol claim for the format. Typical of the acuity of insight contained in these gems is an observation Collett made on the Endemol documentary *Big Brother: Small World*, screened in the UK in early 2002 as a promotional vehicle for applications to participate in *Big Brother 3*. Referring to the romance that developed in the previous series between contestants Paul Clarke and Helen Adams, and the tendency of *Big Brother* contestants across the world to bed and wed each other, he said 'we psychologists refer to it as "The Principle of Propinquity". That is, people who live and work in close proximity to each other tend to form relationships.' So, people are more likely to form relationships with those they spend time with, rather than those they don't. This camera-side analysis is pure junk-psychology, given ballast by the status of its speaker, and is typical of the popular notion of what psychology is, a notion that reality TV perpetuates.

The readiness of figures such as Collett to provide sound bite insights-for-hire brings into question their seriousness as professional psychologists. Mostly, this is harmless enough, and psychologists have long been among the more forthcoming from the ranks of rent-a-quote professionals, but again it is contestants, treated so blithely, who have most reason to feel aggrieved. Stuart Hosking complains of one moment in particular.[31] Collett presented an analysis of Stuart's habit of winking, drolly commenting that it was a device Stuart used to control a group's dynamic, bestowing favour on certain members while excluding others. Hosking was made to look duplicitous when he hugged Penny Marshall, a highly-strung contestant, in a show of reconciliation after an argument. Over her shoulder, he winked at Paul Clarke, who had flirted with Penny in the early days. Where Collett made this appear sinister, Hosking says he was merely affirming that everything was now settled, and Paul need not worry about further tensions. Whatever the truth – and it's in the nature of *Big Brother* that such a miniscule moment can rankle for months afterwards – Collett summed up his little analysis with the tag line 'So Stuart is the biggest winker in the house.' The press thought this pithy sonic echoing of 'wanker' amusing, and the next day saw headlines run with the phrase. Hosking says he hasn't been able to live it down since. He thinks Collett should have been more wary about how he used his authority within the programme, and implies that the analysis was based on a few rushes edited together for Collett to provide a handy voice-over, rather than a result of Collett's own analysis, and that as a trained professional he ought to question the ethics of his role within the production.

In the US, CBS employ Dr Richard Levak as an advisor

---

31. The material in this section is from an interview with Stuart Hosking conducted by the authors.

on their reality shows, chief among them *Survivor*, which exposes its contestants to the harshest mental conditions of any major reality show. Levak spoke at a symposium on reality television held at the 2001 APA Conference, entitled 'Reality TV: Psychology in Prime Time'. Also on the platform was Dr Gene Ondrusek, the first psychologist to be involved in reality television, and Dr Kate Wachs, former president of the APA's Media Psychology Division, in the chair. The session gave an insight into the roles of psychologists in reality television, and many articulated doubts about the ethical boundaries of their involvement. Levak, in particular, was circumspect about the extent to which he and his colleagues are sanctioning a new kind of TV-experiment. He opened the session with the question: 'How many of you as psychologists have a gut bad feeling about reality programs? [About four-fifths of the audience raised their hands] That is just how I feel – and I'm doing it.' He spoke of the tension involved in being employed by a network, and simultaneously protecting the psychological health of the contestants on the shows. The question of the voluntary nature of the programmes was highlighted as a difficulty because, in essence: 'The problem is that contestants waive all their rights, and sometimes losing their dignity is the point of the show. That is complicated for us.' He was aware of the potential conflict between two sets of clients, the production and its participants, saying in his speech 'Agony and the Ecstasy: Psychologists' Involvement in Reality TV': 'We are walking this very thin line between working for the producers but protecting the show by protecting the contestants. It is a very fine line.'

This is the root of the problem with media consultancy on television shows – in whose interests is the psychologist–consultant working? In theory, it could be both, for the mental well-being of the contestant ensures that a show does not disintegrate into scenes of Stanford-like dissolution. In fact, though, the more signs of mental strain a contestant exhibits, the more gripping and 'dramatic' the footage appears to be, and there have been many examples in reality TV of such strain spilling over into dramatic and unstable behaviour. Levak drew attention to the APA's code of ethics (guidelines for all US psychologists to adhere to in their professional practice) and claimed that the involvement of psychologists in reality television shows poses problems for each one of the code's main principles. The principles come under these headings: *Competence*, *Integrity*, *Professional and Scientific Responsibility*, *Respect for Other People's Rights and Dignity*, *Concern for Others' Welfare*, and *Social Responsibility*. One can imagine that any employment with the potential to compromise such worthy objectives could be problematic.

It is open to question how much influence psychologists can have over their paymasters in this terrain, for no professional standards for the maintenance of the participants' welfare yet exist. The psychologists are themselves the chief safeguards, and are being paid to legitimise the production. Taking on this role removes any possibility of real consultative independence, and compromises their ability to exercise the APA's suggested competencies. Like Levak,

Zimbardo is also concerned. He advocates the involvement of psychologists working in the contestant's interest, but believes they should have more than an advisory role, and be given the power of final say: the right to pull a contestant from a show if they think they are at risk of damage.

Dr Wachs and Dr Ondrusek were less concerned, and more effusive about the presence of psychology on television, as seen through the lens of reality television. Ondrusek stressed the benefits of debriefing contestants after their appearances, saying that it helps participants 'expand into the experience and use it in life-changing ways'. If the psychobabble used by contestants in *Big Brother*, *Survivor* and most frequently *Temptation Island* can sound gratingly indulgent, the notion that appearing on a show will help you find yourself, learn how to treat others, or become a better person, is sanctioned by such statements from professionals; the contestants' language of 'making connections', going on a 'journey' within yourself, 'learning not to judge' and so forth may appear to be a crass mangling of the tenets of psychological perception, but it's coming from the top too.

Wachs made an explicit link between reality television and the brand of social psychology exemplified by Zimbardo's study. The Stanford Prison Experiment showed 'how people put in compelling situations can create compelling behaviours' in much the same way, she said, as reality television does today. She spoke with something akin to a sense of wonder at the gift given to us by this new form of observational reality-based television: 'Finding the compelling nature of something, distilling it, and giving it back to ourselves in a compelling form is our nature. It's like turning grapes into wine or *cocaine into crack*' [our italics]. An unfortunate metaphor – an earlier narcotic is distilled and transformed into a cheaper, more addictive, and destructive substance; television and social psychology are mixed to form reality television. It's one thing to marvel at the power of a tool, quite another to justify its use on the basis of that power, and salivating at the psychological power of the medium shows how far the interests of some psychologists involved lie from the welfare of contestants who the producers claim they're hired to protect. Wachs' is a barely concealed glee that reality television has given a new lease of life to social psychology, blessing the discipline with both money and public interest.

There is nothing new in psychologists taking on consultative roles, lending their expertise to law firms, news and documentary programmes, or various other pop-psyche ventures. Reality TV represents a new chance to supplement income. Dr Wachs is hired by America Online as 'Dr Kate', their 'psychologist/relationship' expert. Her 2002 Valentine's Day newsletter provided some typically insightful examples of her work in this field, and gives an indication of just how today's media-friendly psychologists bring their expertise to bear in the world. For those without a Valentine date, the newsletter advised:

> If you've absolutely got no one to call, call the nearest nursing home, and go over and visit with the residents who could use some cheer. For an extra treat, pass out some

inexpensive valentines (usually available at the grocery store).
Let them know they're not alone, that someone cares about
them, too. And in doing so, you will feel immensely valued
and connected, too. *And remember, you are never alone. I care
about you, and I'm sure others do, too.*

It's heart-warming to know that Dr Wachs cares for each of
her hundreds of thousands of subscribers. They are, after all,
her livelihood. She's a good patriot, too, and is sharp to spot
an opportunity to appeal to the national media tone:

If you're feeling sorry for yourself, remind yourself how lucky
you are just to be in this country. AP recently reported that
it is forbidden to celebrate Valentine's Day in Saudi Arabia.
People are forbidden to even wear red, and anyone who wants
to buy a present that has red or suggests V-Day in any way
has to do so weeks before the actual date itself to avoid
detection by the religious police. Offenders, including
merchants who sell such items, are picked up by the religious
police and jailed. Unmarried couples who are caught just
dating are jailed. Men and women are not even allowed to
wait in the same line. Reuters also reported that because the
sexes are so segregated, the most elaborate wedding cele-
brations (what we would call a normal 'wedding celebration,'
with music and food) involve only women! The men celebrate separately in short, tea-and-pop meetings.

So in these troubled times, remember how fortunate we
are to live in the greatest country in the world, with such a
high standard of living and – best of all – with such freedom.
Freedom to express opinions, to practice the religion of our
choice or none at all, the freedom to show our love for our
loved ones, to buy presents of the type we want when we
want them, the freedom to date and choose our own spouses,
and the freedom to move around when we want and with

whom we want without constantly worrying about getting picked up by the police. Can you imagine living somewhere where you can't wear the colour red on certain days?

Founder of The Relationship Center, which acts as both love-therapy centre and dating agency, Dr Wachs has chaired the Media Psychology Ethics/Guidelines Committee. She has also won the APA Media Psychology Division's first Meritorious Award for Outstanding Contribution to Media Psychology. As the spiel on The Relationship Center's website explains,

> she was awarded the honour of 'Fellow' for outstanding and unusual contribution to the science and profession of psychology, particularly in the area of media psychology. This is a prestigious title granted to only a small fraction of psychologists – those who have shown superior, influential, national, cumulative and ethical impact on their field, and who have been judged by their colleagues to merit this symbol of distinction, integrity and respect.

An appropriate figure, therefore, to chair a symposium on the ethics of psychologists' involvement in reality TV. When producers point out that the involvement of psychologists shows how responsibly they look after the welfare of contestants, it's wise to remember that the applications of psychology range from Freudian analysis to 'Dr Kate's Love Secrets'.

Dr Ondrusek is also a clinical psychologist, and he and Levak together constructed the screening process for *Survivor*, which included the MMPI-2, the California Psychological Inventory, the FIRO-B and an assessment for emotional intelligence for stress resiliency. These are established personality tests, but their success depends on their application. In the case of *Survivor*, producers realised that they could use the tests to weed out unstable personalities, but also to find people who would be likely to provide dramatic action. This is a very sophisticated brief for tools that are essentially survey questionnaires, and, however honed the tools are, the resultant casting is sure to settle on reality television's stock, crude divisive pairings – a homosexual living with a homophobe, a small-town white boy with a politically aware black woman. Ondrusek, while not as glaringly populist in approach as Wachs, nevertheless thinks that *Temptation Island* can be beneficial, and galvanise relationships. A man who is concerned for the psychological health of the US's wealthier citizens (he is chief psychologist at the Centre of Executive Health at Scripps Hospital, La Jolla, California), he'd be unlikely to bite the hand that feeds him. Ondrusek has acknowledged that his role is an unusual one, and that 'This is as deep into a media production psychology has gone – from casting all the way through filming and follow-up.'

The APA code of ethics barely mentions the potential compromises that media consultancy poses for its members, and the psychology industry has enjoyed lucrative involvement in some of reality television's precursors, most notably American talk shows, many of which regularly bring on psychologists to assess and advise guests about their situations. Perhaps best known among these is Dr Phil McGraw, who joined *The Oprah Winfrey Show* in 1998. He's notorious for his blunt approach, challenging guests' self-deceptions in harsh, TV-quick barrages of comments, trying to strip the subject of their rationalisations, a technique that frequently elicits extremes of emotional response. This suits the adversarial, charged atmosphere of talk show television, but has little to do with therapy, which is usually thought to require a lengthy period of commitment to be of use. Talk show producers are aware their programmes have been accused of exploitation and callousness, and, after two high-profile murders in the 1990s, are more sensitive than ever to such charges. Rather than tone down the extremity of atmosphere and the harshness of the snap judgments given by their hired authority figures, though, some have sought to compensate and appear more concerned for their guests' welfare by introducing the practice of 'aftercare'. This was the invention of clinical therapist Jamie Huysman and talk show producer Dan Weaver, and works thus: Huysman approaches a treatment centre and describes a forthcoming programme, and the centre is asked if it will provide a free bed for treatment, which can be worth $40,000–$50,000, in exchange for publicity. The compact being mutually beneficial to both parties, they often strike a deal. As Huysman has put it, 'The treatment centre gets heightened public relations and the talk show actually looks like a good person, I mean a Good Guy, which is very important so people don't have to take a shower after they watch.'[32] So now we have talk shows that expose guests to

---

32. *I Was a Talk Show Survivor*, Channel 5 documentary, 2001.

the McGraw brand of accusational pseudo-therapy on the
show, and then flash up advertising messages for treatment
centres before and after the commercial breaks, the very
places that damaged guests are whisked off to after the
show.

Should a guest recover there is the added possibility of an
uplifting 'scars to stars' story on a later edition of the show.
To the audience it appears as though the treatment centres
are endorsing the programmes, whereas in fact all you have
is a traditional, if imaginative, financial arrangement; two
backs, and two pairs of hands. Talk show host Geraldo used
the phrase 'scars to stars' to describe the recovery of one
guest who had appeared two years previously, in 1992,
living in an abusive sexual relationship with her father.
Huysman had been professionally involved in their situation, and when it came to crisis, with the father holding a
shotgun to his daughter after his anonymity had been
breached by appearing on the show, it was Huysman who
regressed him back to his own childhood over the phone
and persuaded him not to kill her. This case was the spur
that led Huysman to team up with Weaver, who worked on
Geraldo, to start aftercare. 'Scars to stars', the promise of a
quick transformation from personal damage to inspiring
celebrity, is the mirage of hope on which the participants
and audience hang, the easy lie, uttered even as a sponsor's
ambulance waits at the back of the building.

Perhaps more so than with the reality game shows, one
can only wonder what motivates guests to appear and share
their familial horror stories. In a US where the people who

are most likely to appear on sensationalising talk shows are also those most likely to have fallen through the social security net, the prospect of appearing on the shows has become attractive precisely because they offer free therapy – increasingly, the health care clinches the deal. Dan Weaver has gone on record to describe his own *Eureka!* moment: 'the light bulb went off ... not only are we giving help, but we're getting more shows out of this'.[33] Everybody's happy.

As is true of almost all organisations and professions, the psychology industry is not very effective at self-regulation. Guidelines remain advisory only, and a look at one set of recently revised guidelines about media involvement shows how flexibility (what might today be called a 'light touch' look at ethics) can be couched in apparently stringent language. The Louisiana State Board of Examiners of Psychologists made an attempt in 1999 to clarify the ethics code in the light of recent media involvement:

> It is clear that media activity is not per se unethical. However, psychologists who practice in this area need to be especially careful regarding potential violation of Ethical Principles 1.03 (Professional and Scientific Relationships) and 1.19 (Exploitative Relationships). Entertainment is frequently the foremost purpose of broadcast mental health presentations but the mental health professional must never allow entertainment considerations to outweigh or dilute the principles of ethical mental health practice. *Data are not readily available on the effects of media psychology on the consumer* [our italics].

---

33. *I Was a Talk Show Survivor.*

This hardly represents a tightening of the guidelines. The text simply advises caution, refers back to the ethics code, and then cursorily admits that no one knows the effects on the public (consumer/patient/contestant ...) of complicity between media and psychologists. Under the appearance of concern for strict regulation of media activities, then, there is nothing but a series of caveats. The agenda behind the above document becomes clear when viewed in the context of its introduction in a newsletter from the APA's Media Division: 'This statement replaces an earlier opinion that severely restricted Louisiana psychologists' media activities.' In other words, the guidelines are redrawn so that psychologists may more easily milk the media cash cow, an ever more lucrative source of wealth and renown since the rise of reality television.

The British Psychological Society's (BPS) guidelines also deal inadequately with media consultation. Dr David Miller of Stirling University complained to the BPS about psychologists who worked on the first series of the UK *Big Brother*, expressing concern that two of the psychologists intended to use the *Big Brother* tapes as research material, and, in a letter sent on 31 August 2000, that

> the section on risk in the introduction to the revised code states that individuals should not be induced to take risks that are greater than they would normally encounter in their life outside the research. To the extent that there are very obvious psychological risks in such a programme, together with the inducements of £70,000, this would seem not to have been adhered to.

Psychology has such a primacy in our society, and we've seen how contestants use the language of therapy and its dilution as psychobabble to justify and contextualise their behaviour and desire for exposure. We hardly need to chart here how central the tenets of psychoanalysis and subsequent forms of therapy have become to our society. Psychologists are revered as those with specialist knowledge have long been in communities, whether in the guise of priests or seers. Whatever the arguments for and against the correctness of those tenets, they are increasingly the shorthand we use to describe and understand ourselves. The involvement of psychologists in reality television shows, and the broad brushstrokes of social psychology that the shows paint for us on our screens, confer legitimacy on this type of entertainment. We see that the guidelines within the profession are at best flimsy, at worst deliberately lax, and that some psychologists are mesmerised by the propulsion of their professional interests, turned into games, into programming across the world, and are only too happy to accept financial reward in return for involvement in, and implicit validation of, a kind of programming which resurrects some of the more dangerous aspects of social psychology, which itself experiments with dark themes of interrogation, incarceration, with manipulation of group character, and runs the risk of taking hold of participants' minds in a manner reminiscent of Stanford, 1971.

6

FRAMES OF MIND

When we remember watching that first season of *Survivor* in the US, or think back to the summer reality fever of *Big Brother 1*, *2* and *3* in the UK, we may recall the hot sloth of contestants sunbathing, some of the more notable challenges, a couple of faces, a catchphrase, an argument or titillating moment. We recollect the various winners, though even they recede as the next series starts up and the human fodder of contestants is recycled. We tend to forget, amidst the images and mundane dialogue, what pressurised atmospheres the shows create for their participants, and our memories collude with the editors in glossing over the days or weeks of tension that lead up to a minute or two of tense screen time in an outburst of tears or anger. Those psychologists who are worried about the shows remember what we forget in the dreary blizzard of cuts and repeats amid the wide-piped cacophony of multichannel TV: that these programmes induce extremes of behaviour the like of which have rarely been witnessed on television, and even more rarely as light entertainment. The reality game shows engender a mentality in their participants far more consuming than any other kind of television has hitherto provoked, for when you create a microcosmic world, replete with roles, rules and rituals, and all existence outside them is blocked out, you create unpredictable and extreme situations, in which people, with alarming rapidity, cease to be as they know themselves to be.

At the extreme end of the genre, some shows are downright cruel, their whole character based around subjecting contestants to harsh conditions they must surmount in order to win prizes. These are the shock jocks of the genre, with none of the psychological interplay between characters, the cultivation of group dynamics over time, that make *Survivor*, *Big Brother* or their imitations reminiscent of the Stanford Prison Experiment. Rather, these shows' direct forerunners are the Japanese endurance game shows of the 1980s and 1990s, in which people were subjected to degradations and pain in spectacles of suffering, with no pretence that the appeal to the viewer was anything other than a delight in cruelty, an acute Schadenfreude.

One such Japanese show was called *Susunu! Denpa Shonen*, roughly translatable as 'Don't Go For It, Electric Boy!', broadcast in 1998–99. It featured an actor who went under the moniker 'Nasubi'. He consented to be locked alone in a small apartment until he was able to win one million yen in cash or goods from magazine competitions, and was allowed to survive only on the proceeds of his winnings. He slowly disintegrated over the period of his internment, and took to pacing naked, muttering. His hair grew unkempt, then wild, and a beard of sorts emerged. Among the prizes he succeeded in winning was a large consignment of dog food, which he ate, sticking strictly to the parameters of the game. Finally, a producer entered the apartment and led him into a small anteroom, the walls of which promptly fell away, and he was revealed, sitting bewildered and naked before a gleeful studio audience, his 'apartment' beside him, revealed as a set construction. He had been in there for fifteen months, unaware that he was even being filmed, and that each week his exploits were winning Japan's largest TV audience.

In the West we haven't gone this far, yet, though we're catching up with a cluster of shows in which cruelty or endurance is *the* theme, rather than one constituting element of the format. *Fear Factor* has run for several seasons on NBC, with occasional special episodes featuring celebrity contestants. It's quick-turnover reality TV, with a different selection of contestants each week competing for $50,000. They're subjected to three rounds of challenges, with the losers eliminated until only one victorious contestant remains.

Some of the challenges are stunts in the extreme sports vein – walking on the wing of a bi-plane, driving a car off the precipice of a multi-storey car park. Others are gimmicks to weed out the squeamish – eating the boiled balls of a bull, for example. But the show has also seen contestants asked to bob for plums in a water tank, the plums sharing space with fifty water snakes and a python; or required to remain still for three minutes with tarantulas crawling over their heads (the spiders' poison not, apparently, neutralised). Though it's a popular myth that a tarantula bite is fatal, there was still the possibility of real harm here. In any case, if the contestants believed, as most do, that such a bite can kill, the cruelty of the game lies in stimulating the 'fear factor', rather than inflicting real pain.

Two recent American shows were based on sickly spectacles of fascist-chic and near mock-ups of torture tactics. 'Near', not because they fell short of simulating torture, but because they sometimes exceeded the simulation and became real torture. The rival shows, broadcast on ABC and Fox in early 2002, were *The Chair* and *The Chamber*; innocent enough nouns on their own, with homely connotations, but in the context of their content and their simultaneous appearances in the schedules, each title infers a utility put to sinister application – 'electric' and 'gas' in turn.

As with much reality TV, the formats of the two shows are strikingly similar, so much so that *The Chair*'s producer filed a lawsuit claiming that *The Chamber* was a direct rip-off, and *The Chamber*'s makers countered with their own suit, alleging various unfair business practices. In *The Chair* contestants, seated in the eponymous metallic, bolt-laden chair, are strapped up to heart monitors. The presenter, the hot-headed erstwhile tennis star John McEnroe, asks quiz-show-style questions, which the contestant can only answer if their heart rate doesn't exceed a certain threshold. The obstacle to this, designed to raise their heart rate above that level, is the administration of various shocks. These aren't electric, but consist of such surprises as the sudden flaring of a circle of fire around the chair, or a trussed alligator being lowered in front of the contestant's face. These may be gimmicks, but they remain terrifying, and the game plays on our assumed delight at a contestant being shocked until their heart rate becomes abnormal.

One of the more curious things about this most curious of shows is that, before entering the chair itself, contestants are subjected to various preparatory tests. Their heart rate is monitored for two hours, they're tested for drugs – such as beta blockers – which would stabilise their cardiac rhythm, and they're exposed to miniature versions of the kinds of stimuli they can expect in the competition proper: a pen explodes in their hand, or they're blasted with sound and a fire extinguisher while reading Shakespeare. It's unclear whether this is genuinely meant to test their capacity to withstand the imminent physical strain, or if it's part of the baroque ritual, or both. Either way, this pre-chair lab testing is a twist on the now standard practice of having psychologists or medics on hand during reality TV productions. Here those professionals seem to function only nominally as protectors of contestants' well-being, their greater role being as administerers of cruelty, a mild echo of the Nazi doctor role of popular imagination, presiding over medical or electrode torture. The safeguards stray before the camera, becoming part of the show, much as the documentary filmmaker once stepped forward from behind the camera into the film.

The Chamber also sees contestants answering questions

while being subjected to extreme environmental pressures, though these are more overtly harsh than those of *The Chair*. At the start of the show, two contestants face off in an initial round, the winner then progressing to the chamber, into which they are strapped, wearing only underwear. Inside, they answer questions while being buffeted with hurricane force winds, or exposed to extremes of heat and cold.

This is torture, used not to extract information, but submitted to for the chance to win a prize. The only agency detaining contestants in *The Chair* or *The Chamber* is their own volition, aiming for a maximum $250,000 or $100,000 in the respective shows. Nevertheless, consensual or not (an issue considered later in this chapter), it is torture for the gratification of the viewing public, or, more precisely, in the hope of ratings and their associated advertising revenue. Fortunately, the public lagged behind the sadistic creativity of the networks in these outlandish examples of reality TV and both shows were pulled from the schedules after a few episodes. The BBC, in a typical misreading of the reality craze (of which more later), bought the format for *The Chair* and ran it, complete with McEnroe, in Summer 2002, toning down the element of cruelty, relying largely on the contestant's nervousness to elevate their heartbeat. As a result, the blood pressure of the audience remained fairly stable throughout.

The big reality game shows, while not solely reliant on the provocation of suffering for their appeal, nevertheless accommodate and thrive on it. We need only turn to *Survivor*, on the highbrow of this lowbrow genre, to see how suffering is embedded into the rubric. The *Survivor* challenges are famously tough, with none of the parlour game trifles of *Big Brother* (where TV challenge high points have seen contestants building towers with sugar cubes, eating sweet corn with a cocktail stick, and, frequently, dressing up). The *Survivor* challenge most popular with the viewers, and most anticipated by contestants, is the 'log challenge', where contestants have to stand on a log supported over water. The player who stays on longest wins immunity from the next vote. Oddly, the Brits are peerless at this challenge. On *Survivor 2* in the UK various contestants knew the precise times of log challenge records around the world. In the first series the winner lasted on the log for over twenty-three hours, standing, in the South China Sea, through extreme heat and then the dark of night, into the next day. In the second series, three competitors lasted twenty-four hours before two agreed to jump off after striking a voting deal with the winner.

Other *Survivor* challenges usually feature a mixture of the physical, or else log-like endurance tests, with the odd quiz-like test so as not to neglect the mind. Necessarily, these involve a certain amount of cruelty, as people do pass out in the heat, or gash their legs collecting spiders from a cave, or else come so close to winning that losing itself is painful (these are very competitive people). One challenge in particular, though, stood out as an example of genuine mental cruelty. The five remaining contestants in the second British series (Spring 2002) were told that a close relative of each of theirs – spouses, partners, a son – had been flown out to the Panama location, and were dotted about the forest. Each contestant had to find all of the five relatives, and remember things about them. So when, for example, Dave came across Johnny's girlfriend, he had to write down four pieces of information about her. A simple enough memory test, then, and one with a great incentive, for the winner, the person with the most correct pieces of information in the shortest time, would spend half an hour in the company of their loved one. The twist was that when each member came across their own familiar, they weren't allowed to speak to or touch them. By the game's rules, then, four of the five, after a month far away from home in a gameworld, hungry and bedraggled, would catch a tantalising and painful glimpse of someone they loved, only to be denied the chance to talk to them. One can imagine the planning session where this idea was raised and refined. What kind of creative can dream up and sanction such a manipulative little game? Did the production personnel who came up with the game ever think the consultant psychologists would object? Viewers were treated to group tears, and to Johnny, who won, hugging his girlfriend on the beach. Later on the night of broadcast the presenter of *Survivor Raw*, a *Survivor* supplement show on ITV2, the ITV network's digital spillover channel, remarked that the embrace had been rather awkward. He should know, being also the presenter of Britain's version of *Temptation Island*, about how people express their love while a camera circles, a few footsteps away. The other four contestants' grim, glum acceptance of the game's manipulation of their most sensitive feelings of absence and homesickness was summed up by one contestant's understatement: 'That was a seriously cruel game though wasn't it?' People will accept much once they've been inside a gameworld for a month, where the social organisation is constructed around competition, even when those challenges constitute a violating and degrading act. Where were the consultant psychologists here? Did they consult guidelines or their own integrity, professional and scientific responsibility, respect for other peoples' rights and dignity, concern for others' welfare, social responsibility – and conclude that, no, these were not infringed by this challenge, the elaborate and sadistic orchestration of which finally provided some twenty minutes of light entertainment on a Wednesday night?

Such challenges are dreamt up freely, more outlandish as each series tries to top the last and retain the ratings and novelty of its first season, as elements of cruelty, many drawn from the repertoire of torture or interrogation techniques, and incarceration (all of which were also mimicked in the Stanford Experiment), are an integral part of the creation of the pocket-world environments in which the reality game shows take place. These elements recur across the shows, all of which betray sinister influences from the darker practices of the last century. Broadly, most of these involve various forms of privation, control, and manipulation of environment. The KUBARK manual, the bible of interrogation techniques used by the CIA in the Cold War, has it that:

man's sense of identity depends on a continuity in his surroundings, habits, appearance, actions, relations to others etc.
Detention permits the interrogator to cut through these
links and throw the subject back upon his unaided internal
resources ... Control of the source's environment permits the
interrogator to determine his diet, sleep pattern, and other
fundamentals.

The reality TV production, acting in the interrogator's role,
does similar things to contestants, prodding their resilience
until they spark into extreme, or at least dramatic, behaviour. They employ the techniques of sleep deprivation, the
illusion of imminent harm, the disjuncture of normal time,
concentration on apparent irrelevancies, the building up
and dashing of hope, and the fostering of distrust and
paranoia. Psychological cruelty has long been present in the
way that we play games, but it's hard to think of another
instance when the formal exaction of great cruelty-methods
honed by states and armies as weapons against their enemies
and the traducers of their codes were grafted onto gaming
in so direct a manner.

At its simplest, the inflicted privation can be the removal
of contestants from their lives, and the restriction of stimuli
from outside the game's environment. In *Big Brother*, if
someone tries to send a message (a phrase on the lawn
written in pebbles, or numbers cut out of paper and stuck
on the wall to represent a loved one's birthday) Big Brother
will tell them to remove the message or face eviction.
Glumly, the contestants comply. Lack of privacy is also an
integral part of reality TV, present in every invasive camera

poked into your tent, or zooming in on your tear-drenched face as you watch a video of your boyfriend canoodling with a stranger. Carter and Endemol point to the surveillance society and proliferation of CCTV cameras across Europe as essential predicates for audience and contestant acceptance of reality TV, although knowing that we're being watched is a very different thing to wanting eyes on you, and their comparison is an ignominious one at a time when questions are being asked about the erosion of civil rights and privacy that public and private surveillance give rise to.

The shows can't exist without this measure of control over contestants, liberty and privacy curtailed so that all angles of focus and interaction are pointed inwards, as lines criss-crossing a group dynamic. Strict administration of that intensity of concentration is necessary to create the conditions, as seen in the Stanford basement, which lead to explosive or compelling behaviour. This is fine – if applicants understand the trade they make, which is actually a complex one, in which they have more liberty than they sometimes realise. *Big Brother* contestants, for example, may leave the house at any time, and at time of writing twenty-one have done so (though, as shown below, the fog of immediate experience within the limited parameters of pocket worlds can obscure their place within the broader reality and dicta of the world outside).

When Charlie Parsons says:

On a desert island you can't escape. In the rules of *Survivor* you can certainly leave for medical and certain other reasons, but in reality it's much harder to do so than if you're in a studio in the West End where you can disappear in your lunch hour and not turn up again and nobody can force you to come back in.

... he puts his finger on a real problem. Without quite saying that contestants cannot simply leave of their own volition, he implies that they need a good reason to do so, and that it's practically difficult. This may be slightly disingenuous – the production can certainly afford to fly relatives out to the location, and one assumes it wouldn't be too hard to arrange transport for unhappy contestants. Further, if anyone leaves any set, no one can literally *force* them to return. Finally, one senses in the recourse to practical difficulties a reluctance to admit that it is within the rights of a contestant to leave if they wish. The original *Survive!* 'bible' makes no mention of any right to opt out once they've opted in; it's just not an explicit option in the way it is for *Big Brother* contestants.

Legally, the actual constraint of liberty can be exercised by state officials on certain grounds only. The Universal Declaration of Human Rights and the European Convention are as one here. Employers, as the productions effectively are to their contestants, cannot truly take away liberty. Of course, a contract can be agreed to whereby the employee agrees to labour under certain constrained conditions, and breaking that contract can prompt legal proceedings, but this is a different thing to the definitive 'can't escape'. They can, and can do so even if they don't require medical attention; they can, if we adhere to human rights

conventions, move freely as they wish, for their own reasons, and, if this breaks a contract – not necessarily the
specifics of a *Survivor* contract – it then may become a legal
matter. Moreover, contract or not, people cannot actually
sign away their own right to liberty and privacy. Certain
conditions, yes; a renunciation of the conventions their state
has signed up for, no. Therefore, a contract that requires
them, effectively, to do so, may not be able to make a
watertight case in law that its terms are reasonable. One of
the European Convention on Human Rights Protocols
contains an item that states 'No one shall be deprived of his
liberty merely on the ground of inability to fulfil a contractual obligation.' So the contestants' liberty is there for
the taking, if they want it, or if they can still, within the
rules and parameters of the game show environment, conceive of it, and they may not, on failing to fulfil their
contractual obligation, have it taken from them again, by
the State. Parsons is here speaking less in the role of an
employer who recognises the limits of his legal responsibilities, and more as the inventor of a world whose rules he
has drawn up, a world in which the declarations of the real
world fade in the face of contractual limitations on liberty.
'Terrible power' indeed, particularly when it's highly
unlikely that most contestants are familiar with their rights
and the limited binding power of a contract, and are the
citizens of a world you have constructed, its laws designed
to subject them to physical and mental extremes.

In addition to the apparent deprivation of liberty, the
shows inflict other privations. Food, particularly, is fetish-

ised in some reality shows in a manner reminiscent of both the privations of internment and the divide-and-weaken tactics of interrogators. The withholding and giving of food at irregular times is a method practised in prisoner interrogations, designed to disrupt the routine of the subject and undermine their sense of normalcy, increasing their dependence on interrogators. In *Big Brother* contestants have to budget carefully for their week's supplies, and are invited to gamble their food money on weekly challenges. Failure brings the loss of a percentage of their funds, demoralising the group and increasing resentment towards the unseen Big Brother construct. In *Survivor* food privation is a key part of the game, wherein the contestants' rations consist of little more than rice. In the first British series there were arguments over whether those with greater body mass should receive more rice. People became so lethargic that they stopped trying to fish, conserving themselves for the physical challenges in which they might win immunity from the next eviction vote. The camp deteriorated into littered and half-broken semblances of their mental states, overrun with rats at night. Towards the end of the series the presenter asked each contestant to weigh themselves after guessing the extent of their weight loss. One had dropped twenty-eight pounds.

Because of the hunger quotient, food is an especially useful instrument in *Survivor*, used to foster group division and sharpen the drama of the contest, just as the giving and withholding of privileges is a classic incarceration and interrogation technique, and is used in the details of some challenges, often as a reward for the winning individual or team. The individual prize for one challenge was a full cooked breakfast, set up on a table on the beach with silver cutlery, toast racks, cold orange juice; the trimmings of civilisation. While the winner of this challenge, Pete, a devout Christian, savoured each morsel of his meal, licking the plate, weeping and thanking God for the sausages, the other contestants looked on enviously. Take the scene out of its game context and you have a picture that epitomises this new form of reality television; a group of people who have spent weeks regarding rat as a delicacy look on as their rival tucks into eggs and sausage, trying not to hate him.

Another stalwart in the repertoire of psychological torture, dealt with in detail in the KUBARK manual, is sleep deprivation, also favoured by reality TV producers. One *Big Brother* task used the disruption of sleep in a particularly unedifying way. A wooden stage was constructed in the garden overnight. Each house member was allotted a signature snatch of music, bursts of which would be blasted into the house at apparently random intervals. Whenever a contestants' jingle was played they had to run to the stage and dance for one minute. They had a few seconds to get in place, and if they failed to start dancing in time, or didn't last the minute, the whole group would fail the task, and thus have less money for food that week. They had to keep this up for twenty-four hours, and were frequently awoken from their sleep, forced to drag themselves outside to the stage. House morale drooped significantly during the course of this task, which the contestants saw as pointless and unfair. The combination of sleep deprivation/interruption with compulsory and routine tasks that served no purpose was a potent means of unsettling them. This challenge echoed the US siege tactic of playing loud music outside, most memorably, Noriega's palace in Panama City. That, too, was designed to disrupt sleep, act as a constant reminder of the subject's restriction of liberty and reinforce the psychological grip of the controlling agency. Loud music was also played in the *Big Brother* house when the producers wanted to drown out the sound of fans or journalists shouting messages over the walls. In Noriega's case, of course, the music was played to coax him out of the building and into the outside world, whereas here it was done to keep the world out of the house.

Big Brother is a clever creature, as it must be to have so insinuated itself into the pop-cultural life of so many nations. It subsumes whatever criticisms are thrown at it. This is why Germaine Greer, an erstwhile critic of the show, can appear on an Endemol documentary about *Big Brother* as a social phenomenon,[34] and why the writers of this book can tentatively be offered a slot on the 2003 *Big Brother's Little Brother*, naysaying from within the belly of the object, as it eats its reaction. So in series three the walkouts were co-opted into the nature of the game, turning glaring evidence of a show apparently disintegrating under its ever harsher conditions into part of the game. One contestant left spectacularly, mocking the show by

---

34. *Big Brother: Small World*, Channel 4, 2002.

pissing in a waste bin before scrambling over the roof, to be last seen trying to leap a wire fence, manhandled by two security guards. Turning weakness to strength, the format now integrates it alongside eviction as a legitimate mode of exit.

The walkouts came as the format, perhaps aware that charges of cruelty and virtual imprisonment could be levelled at it, chose to revel in and accentuate these aspects, rather than cower from them, in its third series. The security around the new set for the house in Elstree studios made it resemble a maximum security prison, and the metaphor was brought into the set itself. Bars were erected, splitting the house in two, one side 'rich', one side 'poor' with only basic facilities; an outside privy and limited hot water. Contestants moved between the sides by virtue of challenges, each game contrived to create suspicion and jealously. By and large, the house members didn't follow suit. They rebelled against the format in petty ways – sneaking between the bars at night, pursing lips and avoiding eye–camera contact when Big Brother called them into the diary room to explain their naughtiness. It was, in fact, a terrible mistake – it inspired depression, grumpiness, resentment, and made the Big-Brother-as-penal system (replete with its own 'three strikes and you're out' rule) look like a pedantic, oppressive and plain nasty TV-regime. There were rumours that Endemol were displeased that their format was turning into a bad joke in Britain, and the bars came down after a few weeks. By making the prison metaphor more real, and self-consciously trying to turn its proximity to incarceration into an ironic virtue, the format started fraying, and the fractiousness, the disconnection it instilled in its contestants, was, for a couple of weeks, dismaying rather than shocking, and for a short while, amid half-formed plans of mass rebellion by the participants, it looked as though the *Big Brother* machine was short-circuiting. The show looked like what it was – a nasty piece of work, and at the same time, ridiculous.

Laying the coercive techniques of reality television and psychological torture beside each other exposes their differences, too: the former is entered into voluntarily, the latter is not. The parallels are there, and reality TV's appropriation of interrogation and torture techniques is a trivialising mockery of their use in the real world. *Most* reality television contestants are able to return to their lives with no more damage than a little embarrassment, some good stories, and the memory of their fifteen minutes of fame. There may be no physical difference between being deprived of sleep in an authentic interrogation and a similar deprivation in the name of entertainment, but the difference between running the risk of losing a challenge on a reality TV show on the one hand, and facing death or pain on the other could not be starker. The pressure must be lessened if the subject knows that the interrogating authority is merely a TV production company, and that they will get out alive. Yet people are affected in extreme ways by the tasks and environments they are exposed to in reality television; and must be for it to be watchable, so the formats walk a tightrope between inducing sufficient pressure to ensure drama, and little enough for the *unreality* of the situation to remain apparent to the viewer. And though they're actually free to leave, the atmosphere engendered by the gameworlds means the essentially voluntary nature of the experience gets obscured in the game's intensity, the environments provided making it very hard to see outside them, as the experiences of some contestants show.

A contestant in the second American series, which broadcast through the events of the 11 September, was called to the diary room and informed of the attacks. She was told that her sister and niece, who lived in New York, were fine, but that her cousin, who worked in the World Trade Center, had gone to work that morning and had not been heard from since. This does not quite represent a new low in television intrusiveness, for news footage has intruded on the process of death many times, but in the context of a light entertainment game show, that the producer remained behind the anonymous lens of Big Brother to tell her, when she could easily have been taken aside into the dignity of privacy is shameful; the horror of that day and the confusion of that woman were used for a moment's dramatic tension. Immersed in the *Big Brother* experience, she chose to remain in the house.

'Nasty' Nick Bateman was evicted from the first British series of *Big Brother* for cheating – he wrote down the names of contestants he wanted nominated and showed them to others. He was also more devious than his fellow residents, making 'psychic' predictions, lying wholesale about the death of his non-existent wife, a military background, and other biographical details. It was plain to viewers that he was not only a schemer, but an erratic and compulsive dissembler. He was popular inside the house, though, until found out and challenged. The showdown was a national event, the talk of pubs and water coolers the next day. When he was evicted the housemates were glum with the sting of betrayal, and there was an atmosphere of collective shock not dissimilar to grief. All the man had done was try to win a game show by bending the rules, but the reaction shows how bonds and betrayals of trust are magnified. Bateman, still pursuing a media career in his 'nasty' character, hired for sinister voiceovers and the like, thinks that contestants shouldn't have been told about the terrorist strikes, saying on the *Big Brother: Small World* documentary, 'You should be kept away from the news and the media, that's the whole point, or one of the points in taking part in this show or experiment or whatever it is.' No previous kind of programming has got people thinking in these ways, as though reality and the show were two worlds, clearly defined and separate, and the former should not bleed into the latter, no matter what. 'It's only a game show', they chanted, less and less sure of this as the days passed.

In the week preceding her eviction from the *Big Brother* house, Narinder Kaur began to feel distant from the outside world.[35] Intellectually, she had always known that entry to

---

35. The material in this section is from an interview with Narinder Kaur conducted by the authors.

the house meant acceptance of a radical break with external
reality, and Brett Kahr warned the housemates before they
signed up that the experience would prove bewildering.
But, she says, you can't know ahead of time what that
seclusion feels like. When she learned of her nomination for
eviction, Narinder went to the diary room, *Big Brother*'s
confessional, and asked if her husband would be there in the
event of her ejection from the house. The voice of Big
Brother replied that there was no contact with the outside
world. Narinder later said: 'I started to wonder: have I got a
husband? Have I got a family? Is there life out there at all? I
knew there was, because people were throwing those tennis
balls over the wall[36] and things, but ... I started doubting
what I had in the real world.'

On one occasion, as happened to most of the housemates
from time to time, Kaur recognised the voice of Big
Brother as that of a production assistant, and greeted her
by name. There was no response, and when Big Brother
spoke again a few moments later, the voice was male – a
quick changeover had been effected. At this point, Narinder felt that reality was breaking down: 'I started to
wonder if there was a world.' It is no accident that these
words are so similar to those of Prisoner 416 after he'd
participated in the Stanford Experiment. Both were

---

36. The tennis balls, wrapped in various messages, were hurled by avid fans and
    tabloid journalists. In the US, people, including evicted housemates, went
    further, hiring planes to fly huge banners with messages over the house. It was
    the absence of these on 11 September 2001 that gave the contestants their first
    inkling that something out there was amiss.

immersed in constructed worlds, where divisions of reality blurred. Reality TV thus uses the same methods as Zimbardo did, but here unchecked, for entertainment, and with, as we have seen, ethical safeguards administered by psychologists whose involvement and efficacy is questionable. Where Zimbardo ended his experiment early for fear of inducing too much mental suffering, reality game shows only end prematurely if their ratings are abysmal. Mental strain such as Narinder's is not always visible, so viewers, who don't have prior knowledge of the personalities on display, may not have a sense of how much someone is being transformed by the game. There have, though, also been some highly visible personality disintegrations in reality television.

The most infamous example of a *Big Brother* burnout came in the second American series, and is a marker for what must be every producer's nightmare: the psychological screenings and background checks fail to identify what *might* be a propensity for violence, a contestant's behaviour threatens to explode the show by bringing real danger and unpredictability into the environment. This was when Justin Sebik, a bartender from New Jersey, got drunk and took to pissing on the windows, then threw wine bottles over the perimeter walls. Later, after flirting with and kissing fellow contestant Krista Stegall, he took a knife from the drawer and said, several times, 'Would you mind if I killed you?' They continued to laugh and kiss, until he held the knife to her neck, saying 'I'm going to slash your throat.' CBS producers handled the crisis by using the Big

Brother voice to ask Justin to go to the diary room (note that he could play with a knife in rather gross violation of the rules one moment, heeding Big Brother's authority the next). After a three-hour interview with the show's resident psychologist, he was removed from the game. He claimed that the incident was a joke. No one was sure whether he was serious, crazy, or just had a lame sense of humour; not the producers, not the viewers online, not Stegall herself, who didn't seem unduly perturbed. Was he only playing at holding someone at knifepoint, by holding someone at knifepoint? How real was it? As John de Mol has said, 'No one knows any more what is true and reality, and what is fiction.'[37] Hours of fun can be had listening to Endemol officials mangle the semantics of 'reality', sounding like Baudrillard might have had he gone into marketing. Stegall, less interested in such distinctions, chose to sue the production for endangering her.

Temptation Island, which turns a partner's behaviour into propaganda against themselves through the edited montages shown to their other half, is adept in undermining the strength of its participants' resolve, spurring them to indiscretions, which are in turn relayed back to the other partner with suggestive editing, creating an escalating circle of misapprehension and misery, provoked and controlled by the production, and usually leading to tears, anger, loss of trust and certainty, and infidelity. Once the contract's signed, the absurd grotesquerie of the *Temptation*

---

37. *Newsweek*, 10 July 2000.

Island world comes to dominate the couples' immediate perception, and the small, created world obscures the one in which they met and become partners. This is reinforced by the group nature of the show. Living with others undergoing the same treatment, contestants quickly tend towards common approaches, common decisions, so one unfaithful act can precipitate a skittle-quick succession of more. In the first British series of *Temptation Island* each member of the female group took one of the single men to bed after a mere few days, claiming that this was not for sex, but to fulfil their feminine need for comfort. They didn't consider it a betrayal when everyone was doing it, the group thus legitimising infidelity and circumventing the need for individual guilt and self-justification. The game and therefore the role of the group enacting the dictates of the game are geared to break your will, and one individual's volition, in the face of collective momentum, proves to be fragile, paper-thin.

We're all familiar with the way groups seem to have a personality of their own. A theatre audience quietens as one, minutes before the performance, although the action hasn't started and no cue has been given; a football crowd swells in one voice. An early analysis of group behaviour came in Gustave Le Bon's *The Crowd*, in which he describes how the individual is psychologically transformed when caught up in a mob. He proposes that the mechanisms of anonymity, suggestibility and contagion transform an assembly into a 'psychological crowd', and the collective mind takes possession of the individual. As a consequence, a crowd member is reduced to an inferior form of evolution: irrational, fickle and suggestible. The individual submerged in the crowd loses self-control and becomes a mindless puppet, possibly controlled by the crowd's leader, and capable of performing any act, however atrocious or heroic. The subject took off anew in the early 1950s. After a half-century in which nations had repeatedly fallen into extreme collectives, the impetus for a new wing of social psychology was, broadly, the question: *could we be Nazis?* Personal identities, merged into a group, become virtually anonymous and normally felt constraints against impulsive or extreme behaviour weaken in the face of collective character. This, in any case, has been the orthodox view in psychology since Le Bon, and was reinforced by the Stanford Experiment and another study conducted in the same era: the classic obedience study made by Stanley Milgram at Yale in 1961–62, which found that, under the authorisation of a presiding scientist, two-thirds of volunteers recruited from the university community would continue to administer electric shocks (no shocks were actually given) to unseen third parties as part of an experiment, even when it appeared that they were causing serious harm, and threat of death.

Milgram's study showed that deindividuation is closely linked to obedience, and the submerging of the individual into a 'crowd mind' can be hastened when the group is headed or overseen by an authority figure. It's rare that contestants rebel against authority in the manner of a Justin or a Brad, or a Danish *Big Brother* household who went on strike, threatened to walk out en masse, and finally negotiated a deal involving family visits and privacy time. So effectively do some reality TV shows create close group environments with controlling, all-seeing authorities at their helm, that we can be baffled, for example, at the way some contestants speak to the anonymous, eponymous Big Brother figure. An Australian contestant, Jemma, was chided by Big Brother for bending the rules, and started bargaining with the authority, asking that they cut a deal whereby she could avoid punishment. Met with intransigence, she started pleading 'Please Big Brother. Please – I have to think of my reputation.' Some contestants manage to remain blithe about the Big Brother figure, while others treat it as an entity, the controlling authority of their gameworld, and, by and large, they obey.

Everywhere in reality television little rituals and collective habits form and envelop a group after its initial days of frenetic acquaintance and establishment of pecking order. The viewer sees a group take on its own personality, almost as though it were a character itself. Often, this is unwelcome to the production. This conformity is true to life – if you take a hypothetical enclosed situation, a group of five people stuck in an elevator for a day, the group would quickly settle into a sequence of repetitive behaviour. There'd be arguments, moments of levity and depression, but the character of the group would take form and remain true to it. Reality TV games do their best to disrupt and unsettle this tendency to stasis, by evicting members of a group, merging two 'tribes', introducing possibilities for conflict at every turn, or having a Big Brother-like overseeing authority, able to manipulate a situation or encourage behaviour from on high, like a Zimbardo or Milgram figure.

Mark Wahlberg (not the movie star, but a namesake) is the presenter of, and authority figure on, *Temptation Island*, playing instructor, club rep, and mediator for the male and female groups. He has enormous power over the contestants, born of the information he holds. They know that he has talked with and overseen the activities of their partners, and in those tense rituals at 'bonfire' the contestants are both wary of, and subservient towards, him. He's an expert in non-verbal sympathy, but can't share information. The bidding up of tension and jealousy is largely in his hands. With his poker face, his deft handling of the game's rubric, and subtle shepherding of the contestants towards sexual paranoia, his approachable but sturdy authority legitimises the premise of the game: to betray your lover. You see people in tears, biting their nails, furious about the snippets of their partner's behaviour, yet they do not challenge him, do not resent his knowing impartiality, but rather look to him for comfort (which he deflects) or with the deference of the helpless. Watching this show, it is discomforting that one cannot readily answer this question: if Wahlberg told the wounded lovers they could punish, with electric shocks, the single who they thought had seduced their partner, would they be more likely to actually do so because the act had been legitimised by the island's authority figure?

What a strange irony contestants are expecting their bodies and minds to remain aware of when going through these tests-for-fun, what an absolutely odd thing it is to be subjected to privation and other techniques designed to undermine you, your confidence, stability of identity, trust, physical capacity, self-control, and all the while to remain perched somewhere above your senses, so that though you expose yourself to duress you remain unaffected by it, because it's not really real. Participants, producers and viewers collude in this disavowal; if we did not, the shows would immediately look horrific: a human zoo, or a torture scene, laid on for laughs.

When questions of exploitation and of potential psychological damage are raised, both producers and contestants usually refer back to the latter group's initial consent. The first series of *Temptation Island* saw one participant stride angrily away from a 'bonfire' where he'd witnessed what he took as evidence of his girlfriend's infidelity. Followed by a camera team, he turned and demanded to be left alone, saying that the evening's discovery was not a matter for the audience, but private, a consideration for his life alone. The cameraman, from behind his hand-held, responded: 'Buddy, the show is your life right now.' This, again, is the Parsons Problem. No television show can literally own a person's life. Yet the mechanics of the situation are such that the environment is all consuming. The contestant was heard later to say that the comment was accurate, because he'd 'signed up for this thing', and therefore had a duty to see it through. What thing? A contract can indemnify an employer against injury, and can specify conditions of labour, but it can't own your life or the keys to your liberty. That is the preserve of incarceration and slavery. Within the world of *Temptation Island*, seceded from the real world, volition diminished by the authority of the production, and by the power of the group enduring the same circumstances, he couldn't see it; if the Parsons Problem is a condition that producers and camera-ops can easily catch, the contestants are prone to it too on their side of the consenting agreement, and it is they who suffer most. That consent, gained with the signing of the contract, is the pivot on which the productions leverage contestants into forswearing their right to privacy, and accepting the cruelties inflicted on them during the run.

Consent has long been a central and fractious issue in the involvement of 'social actors' in programming, and has come to the fore with the proliferation of the use of 'ordinary people' in documentaries, docusoaps and reality game shows. Productions wishing to use 'real people' as characters need to obtain their 'informed consent', and there's been increasing industry-side wrangling over how to define this tricky dyad as the number of social actors, being used for spectacles of greater and greater extremity, has grown. The Broadcasting Standards Commission in Britain commissioned the Stirling Media Research Institute to write a report in 2000 entitled *Consenting Adults?* which examined the practices of a number of reality shows. It also focus-grouped a sample of people to take a snapshot of what the viewing public thought about the issues surrounding consent and the treatment of the people in the programmes, how much they needed to know about the programme, whether they ought to be consulted in the post-production phase, whether CCTV footage that led to an arrest should be subject to the same levels of consent-garnering as a participant in a docusoap, and so forth. The report itself, in the manner of many of the fruits of self-regulation, is cautious and guarded in the extreme. Its concluding recommendation is that broadcasters ought to 'introduce an explicit code of rights for participants ... with information explaining their rights and duties in the television-making process'. The second part of the recommendation was that a shorter, or 'user friendly' version of the code of participants' rights be written, short enough for a two-page flyer which could be handed to every participant.

Timid though the report is, it does touch on some pertinent areas. First, it found that, while most producers seriously considered the ethical dimension of consent (and all were sure to obtain it), it was also legally important to the production, as it relates to the management of intellectual copyright and intellectual property in an increasingly litigious media environment. Further, there's simply no way a production can use, edit, and repeat footage of its subjects unless it obtains their prior consent.

There's an inherent conflict here, as participants' rights and dignity on the one hand, and the freedom of the production to use them for its own ends on the other, both hinge on the consent form. Some forms require the participant to 'cede all control, everywhere and in perpetuity',[38]

---

38. *Consenting Adults?*

while others limit use of the footage to one repeat. As such, the nature of the consent informs the function of the material, as 'contracts setting out the rights and responsibilities between participants and producers, offering the latter a crucial degree of control over their production process, and also legal immunity from retrospective disagreements with participants about how contributions have been or are used'. Unsurprisingly, therefore, the report found a wide variation in the practice of how the signature is obtained, and what it signs away. It argues the importance of the use of plain English in consent forms, but finds that the forms can deviate from this, using legal jargon that make them difficult to understand. Some of the productions took participants carefully through the forms, while others 'produce it 20 minutes before filming is due to begin'. One British *Big Brother* contestant described to us how the pace of the selection process and the garnering of consent can bewilder the prospective participant, making them feel powerless, distant from the awareness that they control one side of the decision. It's impossible to say whether such practice is deliberately coercive or tactical, but it is nonetheless felt as such by some. He described how once you've made it into the second round, the process becomes swift, sudden, dizzying. The only moment when you have control is the initial application, when you fill in the form and make an audition video. After that, the production always calls you, your consent has to be given quickly, and when you are told that you've been accepted there is only a week to prepare, to leave your job and say your farewells. So before you've had a chance to assess what you're doing, you're on television – events sweep you along.

Shortly before the start of *Big Brother UK*, the producers give remaining applicants a talk about the fact that the experience will not be easy, and that the limelight they gain will probably be short-lived and a burden. This is known between contestants and the production as 'the talk of doom'. It is, to the producers' credit, honest about what contestants can expect, and *Big Brother UK* would meet with the approval of the BSC report for informing their participants of the conditions they are likely to face. The mock-harsh epithet, though – 'talk of doom' – immediately makes its function to some extent parodic, and the occasion's proximity to the start of 'the biggest thing that will happen in their lives', as John de Mol describes the experience, means that it would run counter to the momentum of the application process for people to choose to duck out at that late stage on its basis. A rallying pep talk laced with caveats is all very well, but it so resembles a team talk that it enables the production to fulfil its responsibility to inform, while also whetting the appetites of soon-to-be contestants. As one *Big Brother* contestant told us ruefully, they had 'signed up for it, so can't complain'. One finally cannot know how soberly a prospective *Big Brother* contestant can adjudicate their own understanding of the consent they've given. Here, context is all, and it is forever so, in this edited medium, that participants in live reality game shows cannot have any control over the context in which their words and actions will be situated. Thus, when participants complain of the way they were portrayed, that their remarks were taken out of context, as many have throughout the history of factual documentary and entertainment, they do so without recourse, for their first consent does not, and cannot, control how they will be used in the programme if it is broadcast either live or nearly live, when the participants are secluded from the very media which are broadcasting them.

The first part of the dyad – 'informed' – thus becomes very difficult. As the BSC report notes, some shows fulfil their ethical responsibility to inform a subject of what waits in store for them better than others (*Big Brother* would probably score well on this from the BSC's legalistic perspective). It is, though, finally impossible, first to know if a subject is truly informed, and second, for them to be fully informed at all, for neither production nor participant fully knows what is in store for them in these volatile landscapes. The term 'informed consent' has, as *Consenting Adults?* recognises, medical roots. It was established in the 1950s, in the wake of the Nuremberg trials' exposition of Nazi experiments, to establish patients' rights. In the medical profession, the following are the American criteria (the British are broadly similar) for establishing informed consent. It's generally established that the physician must reveal:

- The patient's diagnosis, if known.
- The nature and purpose of a proposed treatment or procedure.
- The risks and benefits of a proposed treatment or procedure.

- Alternatives (regardless of their cost or the extent to which the treatment options are covered by health insurance).
- The risks and benefits of the alternative treatment or procedure.
- The risks and benefits of not receiving or undergoing a treatment or procedure.

The second and third points may be transposed adequately to the participation of a person in a reality show, to how much information they can be given about what they are agreeing to undertake. The other criteria cannot apply: there is no existing condition; the alternative is to continue their lives outside the show; the risks and benefits of such are already known to them. That the term 'informed consent', so laudable in itself, is only uneasily applied to the ethics of television production does not in itself condemn the attempt to apply it in another context, but there is no agreed or even proposed definition within the industry. This is hardly a crime, but as long as it is the case, the notion of informed consent can only ever be a vague one, which deals ineffectually with the relation of power between production and participant, and, in its semantic laxity, weights the deal in the favour of the former, at the latter's expense.

Much of the point of a *Survivor*, *Big Brother* or *Temptation Island* (or even an *Eden*, a *Blind Faith*, *Lost*, *Amazing Race*, *Love Cruise* ...) is that the participant does not know what is going to happen to them. That is inherent in even the game show format (at its most basic: will you win or lose?), but the possibility of being informed is diminished within the elaborate crafting of surprise, challenge and manipulation that these shows rely on. How truly informed consent can be, when the production knows some of the surprises it will spring on the contestants, and does not reveal them, is doubtful. Those *Survivor* contestants, for example, were not informed that people they loved would be flown out on the production's budget to taunt them with their feelings of loneliness and longing for home, and in that case the relatives themselves knew something the participants didn't. The introduction of cash prizes further diminishes the capacity for informed judgement. To apply the medical analogy, it's like informing the patient of the dangers of a surgical procedure and then saying that if they go through with it they have the chance to win a million (or 70,000, 25,000; a sufficiently large carrot to dangle in any case). Much is done under the authorisation of that early, excitedly scrawled signature. The real world, the one in which informed consent was given, diminishes as the microscope of life in the house (or island, cruise ship ...) magnifies all details of the immediate.

Dr Miller raised similar concerns in his complaint to the BPS, but focused on the fact that psychologists, not just the productions, need to 'obtain the disinterested approval of independent advisors and informed real consent from each subject'. He argues that, as some *Big Brother* psychologists have likened the house to an institution, and its inhabitants as being detained, their involvement may contravene 'section 3.5 of the Ethical [sic] principles on the particular duty to obtain informed consent with people who are detained'. Emphasising the difficulty of 'informed consent' he notes that

> one contestant Sada Walkington has reportedly complained that she was kept away from her family when she emerged from the house and that the producers had kept her and the other housemates in the dark as much as they could about what awaited them in the house. 'They didn't really want to let us know what it was going to be like. They wanted to keep us fresh daisy-like and awe-struck' (*Sunday Herald*, 27 August 2000, p. 6).

His complaint was rejected by the BPS, with no explanation given for the decision. He, like a growing number of media and psychology professionals, is outraged about 'the patina of intellectual respectability' that psychologists confer on reality shows.

The untested effect of these situations on those who provide fodder for content has led British psychologist Oliver James to call for a study into the psychological consequences of appearing on reality TV shows. Of course, aside from the anecdotal evidence of severe strain, the obvious difficulty many contestants experience in re-adjusting to a world with less tightly defined parameters than those of the gameworld, to the glare of public hostility and the sodium flare of quick-burn celebrity, it would be all but impossible to make a study which exposes the silent impact on those who have entered, for weeks of their lives, into these public light-entertainment cages. To do so would effectively turn each reality TV show into a Stanford Prison Experiment, albeit one with even more embedded scope for dramatic action.

Perhaps rather than calling for yet further survey questionnaire evidence, it's more suitable to ask people to perform a simple mental trick. Take the scenarios and accounts of what happens in these games as enumerated above (or any of the many examples you may be able to recall yourself) and, as with Pete's breakfast, remove them for a moment from their context as TV entertainment. Keep them in mind in the light of the following words:

> 'No one shall be subjected to torture or to cruel, inhuman or degrading treatment or punishment.'
>
> – Article 5, Universal Declaration of Human Rights, adopted by the United Nations, 1948

7

THE PEOPLE LAB

For all these concerns, one can readily understand the excitement with which some social psychologists regard reality television. Of all the social sciences this wing of psychology sees itself most as a popular science. It is about understanding how we behave, and if 'we' aren't interested in the study of ourselves, it can frustrate the Zimbardos, Ondruseks and Wachs of the world, who see themselves as ambassadors for the study of behaviour.

Zimbardo has said 'My whole life is about giving psychology away to the public'.[39] It must be exciting to be able to turn on a television and see groups of people in situations strongly reminiscent of the type of social experiment conducted in the late 1960s and early 1970s, which it has not since been possible to recreate. Ondrusek expressed the star-striking allure of the genre when he said at the APA symposium: 'Reality shows are in their infancy. Entertain-

---

39. Philip Zimbardo, quoted in an article by Betty Mason, <www.stanford.edu/dept/news/report/news/may2/zimbardo-52.html>, 1 May 2001.

ment since Sophocles has recounted and acted out dramas. This has been the model for entertainment up to the present day. This is the first time we have been able to create a new form of drama by creating contexts for compelling behaviours.'

As the influential creator of a template 'pocket world' Zimbardo perches over the reality game shows as he does over the history and legacy of social psychology, and now, as APA president, over the largest organisation of psychologists in the world. While he acknowledges the excitement he himself has felt about the genre, he is also more circumspect than Wachs and Ondrusek, his enthusiasm countered by scepticism as to where the trend will lead. He is wary that 'the current crop of reality TV has to push the limit because audiences get jaded',[40] and is suspicious of what the true appeal of the shows might be, that 'what you're showing is the worst of human nature', with a ready supply of 'people willing to degrade themselves just to be on television'. He claims that the motivation of instant celebrity is growing with every passing season, as the reality game shows become part of the landscape: 'in the first *Survivor* series the people who dropped out first were very upset, in the second series they were not upset at all, they were happy to be the first on late night television, and I know this because I know the psychologist who was doing the debriefing'. So, for Zimbardo, reality television takes

---

40. Unless otherwise indicated, the quotes from Zimbardo in this section are from an interview conducted by the authors.

some of the techniques of his 1971 study, retains some of the fascination of watching people in compelling situations, but sheds the educational and pro-social intent, leaving a genre of shows which 'are the extreme of Western individualism run amok'.

A true populist, he's nevertheless no stranger to using television to illustrate psychological theories. He has produced a series of videos with Allen Funt, late presenter of that other early forerunner to reality TV, *Candid Camera* (released by McGraw Hill), which excerpt moments from the show to illustrate basic themes and principles in social psychology. Zimbardo's website[41] promises that when students watch these they will 'learn while they laugh' (which must be better than 'laugh while they learn'). Zimbardo is eager to credit the debt of influence that both reality television and social psychology owe to Funt, saying that *Candid Camera* is for him the model of how to convert the psychology of live situationist experiments into entertaining, yet illuminating television.

He has worked as chief scientific advisor and onscreen analyst on a reality television programme, produced by LWT and shown in both the UK and US in 2000. It ran over three hour-long slots and was quickly forgotten, being the epitome of the kind of serious observational reality television that Zimbardo favours, and therefore rather dull viewing by the standards of its kin. *The Human Zoo* took a

---

41. <www.zimbardo.com>. See also <www.prisonexp.org> for Zimbardo's own detailed narrative of the Stanford Prison Experiment.

group of twelve volunteers and housed them together for a period of three weeks. They were filmed by a three-person video crew and hidden cameras, and subjected to a series of situations which Zimbardo analysed for the benefit of viewers.

The experiments were designed to illustrate various psychological processes, and for each one there was a cutaway to a similar real-world experiment, or to archive footage of personnel offices, shopping malls, trains, businesses, schools, sporting events and the like, where parallel behavioural phenomena could be observed. Zimbardo was the main creator of the situations the participants were placed in. He based each of these on one or a series of classic psychological studies. One such experiment saw the group split into two teams, each issued with identifying sweaters, one red, bearing the letter 'A', the other blue, marked 'B'. Zimbardo then observed how the group dynamic altered, the hitherto harmonious mood devolving into fractiousness. When a member of one team fraternised with someone from the other, it was observed how she was treated to hostility from her own team, and then came to align herself with her own group. This was typical of the kind of benign bite-sized social experiments contrived on the show. Zimbardo is wary of experiments with a harsher edge, having set the standard thirty years before.

In a contribution to a psychology internet discussion group, Zimbardo, while exhorting the list members to watch *The Human Zoo*, wrote that

> it represents the best in Reality TV, when done responsibly and with respect for the intelligence of the audience. What the current crop of reality tv [sic] shows is that human behaviour is fascinating to observe. I believe that is even more true when experts help the public give that behaviour meaning and focus their observations, and this is what the Human Zoo series attempts to do.

The implication is that the show represents a rebuttal to glamorising, sensational reality TV such as *Survivor*, and is the progenitor's attempt to reclaim some of the integrity of social psychology-gone-TV as expressed in reality television.

The most concerted attempt to produce a reality TV show which would ostensibly fulfil Zimbardo's wish that it return to what he finds most fascinating about it – scientifically valuable, educational, observation-based, and in the hands of professional experts – was made in December 2001 in a collaboration between the BBC and two British universities, and was broadcast in May 2002 in the UK. In fact, it was so close to Zimbardo's interests that he expresses reservations about it, and is suspicious of the BBC's motives, asserting that, hoping to get the same results as the Stanford study – 'behaviour running out of control, people dominating other people' – they were more interested in the entertainment quotient than the scientific or educational value. After all, his fingers had been burnt before; the BBC planned to reprise the Stanford Prison Experiment as a reality television show called *The Experiment*.

The Experiment embodies the themes of the second half of this book. It features the close involvement of psychologists in a reality TV show and is as such a cautionary tale of what happens when television and psychology jump into bed, it is a prime example of a manufactured pocket world with all its attendant harshness and effects on its participants' personalities, it shows the gulf of understanding between popular conceptions of psychology and its reality, and features, because of its nature, the most Stanford-like conditions yet seen on a reality TV show, making explicit the link between the study and the television genre. It was also an example of the BBC trying both to fulfil its public service remit and to score a reality TV hit, something it had failed to achieve before.

It was the BBC who approached the two psychologists – Dr Steve Reicher of St Andrews University and Dr Alex Haslam of Exeter University – with the idea of rerunning Stanford. Though both men deny that the show is straightforward reality TV, there is little doubt that the proposition was attractive to the BBC because it represented a way of making a reality TV programme – with the pocket world, the personalities in close proximity in tense surroundings, all the contrivances of the various experimental methods employed, and the *Big Brother*-style blanket surveillance – which they could claim was within their public service remit, being educational, scientific and backed by the authority of two universities. The BBC has always had trouble with reality TV, and is one of the few popular networks not to enjoy a substantial hit with recent forms of the reality genre, though it has done well with docusoaps and many lifestyle formats that make use of real people/social actors. Their *Castaway* was shown before the British versions of *Survivor* and *Big Brother*, and should have enjoyed a head start in a country where tantalising stories had for months trailed a new European TV craze called 'reality TV'. Its format, and bewilderingly inept scheduling, were typical of the BBC's problems in this area. A group of hardy volunteers agreed to spend a year on a remote Hebridean Island (one hears Parsons snorting derisively), with minimal resources, and to be filmed for the duration. It was reality TV without the games or glamour. Early months were dogged by bad weather and illness. There was delight in the tabloid press as participants refused to start their year's stint until they were over their colds and had finished constructing their shelters. The show was caught halfway between being a serious human-interest reality series (though there was no real study involved, no perceptible *point* to it, so the show could never tag itself in viewers' minds as being *about* anything) and a straightforward reality TV show, focusing on relationships between inhabitants. *Castaway* was just building an interest in the nation, the stories had just started to turn to the participants and their group dynamic (a practice run for the summer of 2000's *Big Brother* press circus), when it disappeared from the schedules – for *months*. It returned after the first summer of *Big Brother*, overtaken by reality shows that knew what they were, by which time no-one was watching.

Wary of charges of 'dumbing down' and reluctant to plough a headline sum of licence payers' money into big cash prizes, *The Experiment* provided an appealing vehicle with which to try again, to twist reality TV to deliver the thrills and yet maintain the high ground of standards. It also reeked of that other quality beloved of producers – controversy. The methodology of the show, though milder, was to be based on the Stanford Experiment and given what happened in the original, the production was bound to attract interest, and raise questions about potential exploitation of citizens at the hand of state-owned television. Furthermore, the tag line – fifteen people incarcerated and divided into guards and prisoners – is concise and memorable, avoiding the vagueness of the *Castaway* project.

To its credit, the premise was not a fudge. Where *Castaway* could only tenuously claim to be educational, the BBC gave Reicher and Haslam full control over the design of the experiment, anxious that it double up as good TV and a serious study. When they told the BBC they were not interested in merely rerunning Stanford, but in conceiving a new experiment, analogous to it in many ways but also crucially different, the corporation listened, and gave them time to construct it. In the end, they spent nine months designing the study, during which the BBC kept people on the payroll for the show. Throughout the production, pre- and post-, the BBC did not pressure the two psychologists to bend the study towards increased entertainment or dramatic extremes. Both parties wanted to get it right.

One senses, speaking to Dr Reicher, that he was motivated by the urge to redress some of the lessons learnt, in his view erroneously, from Stanford. There are two perceptible strands to this – one political/moral, and one scientific. Reicher speaks of Zimbardo's study as 'part of the zeitgeist, part of the way of understanding who we are'.[42] His and Milgram's studies have shaped the way we think about our nature. Even if we don't know about the details of the studies, they are influential parables, and just as 'we live in a Freudian century and are Freudian subjects, whether we agree or disagree with Freudian theory' so the Stanford study shapes our collective understanding of how we behave. The parable, he believes, is not an encouraging nor accurate one. Much like that literary parable, *Lord of the Flies*, Stanford carries a brutal message: essentially, we are brutes, whose social identities are paper-thin, who will transform under pressure. Within a group set away from the world and our normal roles within it we will, on the one side, become brutes capable of inhuman behaviour we couldn't previously conceive of, and on the other capitulate swiftly to power and authority when subjected to it. As Reicher puts it, the study has given rise 'to the view that all you need to do is to put a uniform on people and they either turn to tyranny or they become passive victims. We felt that was a dangerous message, gets rid of any human agency. On top of that it could be read as saying I was only following orders – an unconvincing and uncongenial message.'

---

42. The quotations in this section from Reicher are from an interview conducted by the authors.

This is a sound-bite commentary on Stanford, but is accurate, and very similar to Zimbardo's own summary: 'really after the second day most of them [the "guards"] were totally into the role ... you put on the uniform you put on the reflective sunglasses, you take a Billy stick, you take the handcuffs and you're a guard'. Also, and emphasising the parable-like nature of these live situational experiments: 'What we see is that if you put good people in an evil place in a matter of days the external environment begins to consume the individual, you become the place, the place becomes you. It's really a modern version of Jekyll and Hyde without the chemicals.' Not so, says Reicher – personality is not passive in this way, and where Zimbardo and Milgram put the emphasis on obedience, tyranny and capitulation, Reicher is interested in the possibility of resistance, and speaks, one senses, for a model of human behaviour wherein we tend towards order in groups, but within which we also like to function pro-socially, collectively, and resist attempts to curtail our ability to do so.

The other problem Reicher has with Stanford lies in its methodology and subsequent dissemination. For him, Stanford poses as a scientific study, but the findings were never written up in the conventional way, nor formally published. Instead, you have Zimbardo's film *Quiet Rage*, and the information on the website. He thinks the lessons of tyranny that Zimbardo drew don't fit with the facts – only one guard was particularly brutal, the so-called 'John Wayne' of the group – and that 'resistance is written out of the history of the study'. Zimbardo's many interventions into the study as prison superintendent shaped it, leading to a confusion of roles among the volunteers, and making the methodology suspect. Damningly, Reicher says that 'ethically it's a quite remarkable thing to do – you could argue it virtually constitutes illegal imprisonment – akin to kidnapping'. So *The Experiment* was conceived as a redress rather than a repeat, a rebuff at the beginning of a new century to the assumptions of the old.

What they have in common, though, and share with the producers of the reality game shows, is an appreciation of the power of the constructed and observed miniature world. Reicher, though, was motivated not by audience share but by the opportunity to challenge the essentialist assumptions of Stanford: 'There's a very useful purpose in being able to create worlds and seeing how they transform people … being able to systematically create and observe histories is quite powerful in contesting essentialisms which sadly are so powerful in psychology.' Social psychology these days concentrates on personality questionnaires, which produce static results, isolated snapshots of traits and tendencies, which may serve the interests of the screening process for a reality show, but are of limited use. Reicher speaks of the importance of being able to observe people in the social world over time. In order to do so the psychologist needs to 'build an environment, a social world over which I've got total control and can keep people in over a period of time. It's breathtakingly expensive and in part the BBC gave us the opportunity to do that.' They couldn't have done the experiment without the television money, and nor could they have monitored the participants so closely without the technology and techniques pioneered by *Big Brother*. Thus, the success of those other powerfully resonant pocket worlds, those of reality TV, made the study possible.

The Experiment was not a ratings success. Between one and two million viewers watched each of the four episodes on BBC2. Like *Castaway*, it suffered from ludicrous scheduling, the first two episodes appearing on consecutive evenings, and the last two in the same slots a week later. Eight days, as schedulers at networks who have successfully hosted a reality show will tell you, is not long enough to build a following or let word of mouth spread. It was also not long enough to do the events of the study justice, or to spin out the complex, quick, evolving drama that took place. This was typical BBC bashfulness, and reeks of last-minute nerves, for the production was a big project, involving, as mentioned above, the best part of a year, the construction of an impressive simulacrum of a prison in a West London studio, *Big Brother*-like complexities of surveillance, and a protracted editing job. Moreover, the show had gathered an air of mystery around itself, with press articles for months beforehand, rumours of unhappiness amongst the participants, shock that reality TV entertainment was being squeezed from a rerun of Stanford, and, when it emerged that *The Experiment*, like Zimbardo's study, had been ended prematurely, an expectancy that we would see similar ghastly events taking place. The broadcast was delayed, and it was clear that something had gone wrong.

The events inside the prison certainly provided enough material for a hit, and the close observation of the participants as seen in the final cut gave those who watched more moments of sheer reality drama than have been seen in any series of *Survivor*, *Big Brother*, *Temptation Island*, *Fear Factor* or the rest. For sure, *Airport*, the hit BBC reality docusoap, had nothing on *The Experiment*. Reality TV is worth talking about at length not just because it provides a good vehicle to examine the state of the international TV market, with its template formats, magpie habits and global reach, or because it represents the epitome of the slide of objective factual programming into a morass of the mundane details of first-person trivia, or because it raises questions about the ethics of psychologists hitching a ride on the gravy train, or even because it exposes its human fodder to extreme and dangerous conditions in the name of entertainment, but also because at its best it does throw up moments of genuine fascination, compelling situations and behaviours, indeed, moments where the chorus of the group, the buckling or transformation of individual behaviours, the pressures of the environment, the skill of the editing, the parable-like corollary between the events seen and those of the larger world, and the opportunity for us to watch, in detail so vivid we can see the glistening of eyeballs before the tears start, combine to deliver a televisual and human spectacle that is powerfully new – a people laboratory, made for TV. Putting aside the ethics of how the lab is built, how the experiments within are observed and for what end, and how we peer into it, noses at the window,

The Experiment contained moments of captivating reality TV par excellence.

Reicher claims that 'we [psychologists] build theoretical models in the image of our experiments'. They also have a tendency to build experiments in the image of their theoretical models, so where Zimbardo found passivity and tyranny, Reicher and Haslam found resistance to authority, and much more. Their guards couldn't function as a coherent unit, and were largely uncomfortable with their power. The prisoners, though, revelled in the underdog role, pushing the boundaries of their incarceration ever further, until the prison system, the very construct of the experiment, collapsed. They were marshalled early on by the introduction of a new prisoner, a retired trade union negotiator, who, within hours, took the mischief of a pair of prisoners and the weakness of the guards, and transformed it into social organisation, negotiating a host of privileges and changes in conditions, winning the loyalty and respect of both groups, and using that power discretely and with transparent fairness. Within a day he had politicised the set-up, educating the prisoners in the realities of class conflicts, and yet uniting both groups on common grounds as 'employees' of the production, who had made the set uncomfortably hot. He suggested that both guards and prisoners complain about these working conditions. When one prisoner countered that they couldn't do it because they'd signed up for the study, the skilled negotiator, quick as a snap, told him that he had signed a contract to take part in an experiment, not to suffer under unfair living conditions. Recognising that his peers were thus suffering under the Parsons Problem, he quickly exposed its artificiality, and also therefore that of the experiment's prison setting. If Reicher complains of Zimbardo's interventions shaping the course of the Stanford Experiment, the introduction of this new prisoner was bound to mobilise the prisoners, to realise their capacity for peaceful resistance. They took him out of the experiment after a day, telling the other participants that this was for health reasons, and explaining to him that critics of the study might be able to say its validity was undermined by the presence of one strong personality (though in fact this had already, by that point, occurred – if Zimbardo had inserted a new prisoner schooled in techniques of formal resistance, this would surely have altered the events of his allegory of tyranny). One canny prisoner, 'Mr Bimpson' (the prisoners and guards were to be addressed by title and surname, a mild nod to the numbering of the Stanford study), dismissed the pretext, 'It's nothing to do with health – he's raised the rabble and now . . . '. Bimpson had been the first to spot the political parable of the situation, relating the story of *Animal Farm* to an inmate on the first day, pausing before saying, hunched over his tattoos, with his broad gleam and Liverpudlian eloquence, 'And then the pig said "We are all equal, but some of us are more equal than others." ' Later he said to his cell-mate, 'It's a microscopic world – what we have here is a military junta – we're trying to take over the ruling class. Now if you multiple each of us by one hundred, or one thousand, you've got every revolution in history going on in here.'

With guards failing to discipline inmates who openly flouted their authority, the prison system collapsed and was replaced by a commune. It lasted a day. Bimpson, commandeering the energy and will of the two chief troublemakers, proposed that they secede from the main group, then take it over. The night before the planned coup he slept for an hour, staying up in what had previously been the guards' mess to write a speech he would deliver to the group. He would periodically stare at the camera perched high in the corner, perfectly still, challenging the experiment's presiding authorities, Reicher and Haslam. He told such a camera that they would need military uniforms with black sunglasses – junta wear.

The speech was mesmerising. His lieutenants stood or lounged in the guards' surveillance booth, and the others all sat at the prisoners' meal table. They didn't walk away or reject him as one individual, but were held in his spell as he argued that they needed strong leadership (himself), and insulted their lack of will, the weakness of their nascent communal structure. As Reicher says, 'It was like watching Weimar Germany ... it was like seeing the beginnings of fascism.' The psychologists ended the experiment, a day and a half before its scheduled conclusion. As Reicher explained, the confines of the experiment could not support the kind of social organisation that was imminent, one that would necessitate the viability of real force. They wouldn't play with fascism, and, despite their theoretical models, the prospect of tyranny had finally torn through the parameters of their constructed setting.

This was an experiment and also a television show. As both, it was an acute example of a pocket world, and proved to be as totalising as any seen in psychology or reality TV. Bimpson never lost sight of the fact that he was in a constructed world, a fake prison, and yet he did try to take it over. As such, his behaviour was neither mere role playing nor entirely authentic. Rather, it was a dual consciousness, much as Narinder displayed when she both knew perfectly well that the real world existed yet doubted it, much as prisoner 416 was both a college student and a suffering prisoner. The awareness of playing a role does not occlude the possibility of ones' actions and feelings within that role being as authentic as any other; the game is not removed from life, for its duration it *is* life, both a pretend world and the real world. The adoption of role is not cut off from reality, but is something that happens throughout real situations, 'real' insofar as they occur in the larger world, but equally constructed, assigned, coercive. As Zimbardo puts it:

> [the awareness of playing a role] was there at the beginning of the Stanford Experiment, only because it's so alien – you ask a college student to be a prison guard – and I would bet for example, that if there were videos of Nazi concentration camps, I would bet the first week of a Nazi concentration camp we'd take somebody and put him in this position that he doesn't have any training in [and he'd show] the awkwardness of getting into a role.

The psychologists came across poorly in *The Experiment*.

They too were playing a role, that of 'TV psychologists', one that, as we see from the *Big Brother* psyche soundbites, makes clever people look silly. Reicher and Haslam's part in the drama was reduced to them sitting in front of a bank of monitors, commenting on the action in snippets only slightly more perspicacious than those of the 'principle of propinquity'. During the final collapse of the commune, they were seen both munching from brandless packets of crisps/chips, looking for all the world like two men viewing a rough cut of their first feature film, which, in a sense, they were. Reicher explains how difficult the editing process was, the translation of serious psychological arguments to a TV setting where 'the argumentative context for the audience is completely different to the argumentative context for us and for why we did the study'. The popular misconceptions of what psychology is and what psychologists do, a misconception that the Colletts and Wachs of this world, with their 'spurious academic justifications' (Reicher again) perpetuate, proved to run so deep that there had to be an ongoing instructional process between the psychologists and production team. Reicher and Haslam, like the participants, were filmed constantly. They would, at times, in the canteen for example, discuss body language, how the prisoners were dressing – the trivial minutiae of observed behaviour – much as one gossips at any workplace. This tittle-tattle, though, appeared in early edits of the show, and Reicher and Haslam had to educate the production that, no, this isn't what psychologists actually do, so the process by which they settled on the final format was arduous; that it still looked so contrived indicates the near impossibility of taking the best of reality drama and mixing it with the seriousness of a subject more suited to a lengthy expository documentary. Again, the BBC were patient through the editing, and it is this, together with the dismay of some participants at the way they were portrayed, that delayed transmission (note that consultation with participants in the editing stage here exceeds the level of consultation between production and 'social actors' found in most of the shows used in the *Consenting Adults?* report).

Whatever the scientific value of *The Experiment*, it was terrific reality TV, for it took those elements that the genre borrowed from social psychology and distilled them back, applying also the techniques, technology and editing skills of the TV genre. Much of the psychological value was lost in the translation to the small screen, but in any case the power of such live experiments in the world, as seen with Stanford, lies in their power as parables, and that, certainly, was present. It was in the end a parable about the dangers of power, the volatility of social organisation, the tendency for demagogy to rush, like water, where it can, and as such was a rare thing in contemporary television. It was, it must be said, therefore also somewhat pat, but then so are *Animal Farm*, *Lord of the Flies*, even the parable of The Good Samaritan. *The Experiment*, as a reality show, was honest about the fact that it was dealing with dark undercurrents – incarceration, interrogation, power, abuse, tests of human behaviour similar to those conducted by Zimbardo in an age where the psychologist could set up and run a prison in a university basement. As science, it oughtn't be judged by its TV incarnation, and the findings are yet to be published – a group of people behaved in certain ways, under highly controlled and contrived conditions; the extrapolations, the corollary made between that pocket world and reality at large, will be debated in their specialist arenas. Those other Zimbardos, who set up their own, producer-controlled worlds, whether in the guise of a house, a cruise boat, or a remote island in the South China Sea, ought to be very careful, as they probably don't quite know what they are playing with. If they do, then they, and those consultants who help them run their game-kingdoms, should know better, for the people who go into these shows may have the potential to be a Prisoner 416, or, at worst, a Sinisa Savija.

8

REAL POLITICS

By mid 2002, reality TV had lost its gloss of novelty, and was haemorrhaging viewers in the US. CBS's *Survivor* continued to pull strong ratings, though fans who'd been watching from the start complained that it seemed stale. This was hardly surprising. Series 5, *Survivor Thailand*, started filming less than two years after the format first aired, and such a breathless pace was bound to leave the show a little tired. A new sub-genre of celebrity docusoap emerged, pioneered by MTV's foray into the home life of Ozzy Osbourne, which won the music network their best ever ratings and some much needed kudos for finally running a show that attracted some attention. In Bazalgette's phrase, the locusts were quick to start swarming. Anna Nicole Smith, *Playboy*'s 1993 playmate of the year and wife of billionaire J. Howard Marshall, soon signed up for a similar extravaganza, as did diva and prolific divorcee Liza Minelli. Various rappers, E-list celebrities and icons such as Courtney Love were quick to invite the cameras into their homes too, noting that Ozzy Osbourne's backlist had received an astonishing boost from his docusoap exploits. But a succession of reality game shows such as *The Chair* and *The Chamber* (see above) flared and died like burning newsprint, though the former was exported to the UK, where former tennis star and furious young man John McEnroe did a pretty good job of presenting it.

Just as the genre was beginning to seem moribund, yet newer variations were spat out of rushed development and into the headlines, with the irresistible force of bad ideas whose time had come. Audition show *American Idol*, which sought to find a popstar, became a massive hit, following successful outings in Australia, the UK and much of Europe, while dating game shows *The Bachelor*, and the beautifully named *Bachelorettes – IN ALASKA!* mesmerised the nation with their pursuit of true love. But it was the 'war against terror' that provided for the most ominous developments in the field, lending an Orwellian cast to reality TV far more troubling than Endemol's use of the *Big Brother* motif.

In the aftermath of 11 September, with Middle America rallying behind the troops and the wider West in compliant shock, a succession of military-based reality shows, known as 'militainment', entered production. Since US troops began operations in Afghanistan, the national press had struggled with the toughest reporting restrictions in the history of warfare. For months after US bombing raids began on 7 October, the Department of Defence allowed reporters no access to service personnel, prohibited journalists from travelling to neighbouring countries where the

US was establishing airbases, and refused to even confirm troop deployments. Not only was the theatre of operations under an effective press blackout, but the mood of belligerent national unity gave rise to what much respected anchorman Dan Rather condemned as a culture of self-censorship. He likened the treatment of 'unpatriotic' journalists to the Apartheid-era South African practice of necklacing – placing a burning tyre round the neck of an alleged traitor, causing slow and agonising suffocation as the skin melts beneath chemical flames. Those who deviated from unquestioning support of the Bush administration were not subjected to physical torture, but the new rules of the game were clear. Shortly after 11 September, Bill Maher, host of ABC's *Politically Incorrect*, opined, in an offhand way, that US pilots dropping bombs on guerrillas who would fight to the death hand-to-hand might be *perceived* as cowardly. Within twenty-four hours, advertisers were threatening to pull their spots. The show was axed a few months later.

The Pentagon, though, was not withholding co-operation from all quarters of the media. The PR catastrophe of the Vietnam war had taught the government to be wary of journalists, but the poll-conscious Bush administration realised the necessity of maintaining public support for military action. When Hollywood golden boy Jerry Bruckheimer, producer of such films as *Top Gun*, *Pearl Harbour* and *Black Hawk Down*, approached the top brass with a proposal for a military reality series, *Profiles from the Front Line*, it was endorsed by the men at the very top. Both the

Secretary of Defence, Donald Rumsfeld, and the Vice-President, Dick Cheney, were alleged to have approved the show. Offering access to Hollywood's finest was seen as no threat to national security. In the words of an unnamed Pentagon source, quoted on the British programme *Newsnight*: 'The advantage of working with entertainment producers is that these guys are a lot less likely to go to Baghdad and get the flip side.'[43]

Bruckheimer, co-producing with Bertram van Munster (whose credits, tellingly, include lengthy stints on *Cops*) was frank about the purpose of the show, calling it a 'salute to our military'. Although the Pentagon retained pre-screening rights, Bruckheimer insisted that they did not have formal editorial control, a credible enough claim, given his admitted lifetime support for the Republican Party in general and the Bush dynasty in particular. Asked by the *Guardian*[44] if the show would screen footage of 'some human rights violation, or some mammoth military cock-up', if the production stumbled across it, Bruckheimer responded that it would. He went on to qualify this response, saying hypothetical US atrocities and incompetence would be included only if the Pentagon did not 'consider it sensitive', adding, 'yeah, we're not looking for that'. In truth, the *Guardian*'s question was a little absurd; the Pentagon could withdraw all access to military personnel if they found a sequence or episode to be objec-

---

43. Quoted by Madeline Holt, *Newsnight*, BBC2, 16 May 2002.
44. *Guardian*, 22 May 2002.

tionable. The same threat, implicit in the logistics of filming *Cops*, has ensured a flattering, when not downright glorifying, portrayal of law enforcement for over a decade. Moreover, Bruckheimer wished not only to salute the military – he felt patriotically obliged to screen nothing that might deter potential recruits: 'I think we look to the military as something that protects our shores ... and I think you want the best and the brightest protecting your home and family. We also want to attract the best and the brightest to the military, so we don't want to make them look terrible.'[45]

Rather, and many others in the mainstream press, were scathing about the show, condemning the 'Hollywoodisation' of the military. 'This isn't war', Rather told the BBC's *Newsnight*. 'What you're seeing is a made-for-TV reality series – it's someone's idea of war.' Erik Nelson, maker of the History Channel's *Nazi America: A Secret History*, though a firm supporter of the US effort in Afghanistan, questioned the capacity of the shows to be anything other than propaganda: 'everyone who makes a reality show knows there is always some performance involved. And with the obligatory Pentagon public information officers looking over their shoulder, that reality could become even more unreal.'

Profiles from the Front Line was not the only khaki-clad reality show of the period. CBS screened the first episode of the ill-fated *American Fighter Pilot (AFP)* in March 2002.

---

45. *Ibid.*

Shot before 11 September, and produced by Tony Scott, director of *Top Gun*, the show was repackaged in light of the 'war on terrorism', with a notable lack of subtlety. Each episode opened with a quick reprise of recent events, showing the planes striking the twin towers, followed by a clip from one of Bush's 'war against evil' speeches and the image of the stars and stripes, in case, presumably, anyone was still missing the point. Despite this potent appeal to the national sense of victimhood and a human interest angle on the difficulties faced by pilots in maintaining family lives, *AFP* belly-flopped, gaining only 4.2 million viewers on its first outing – a third of the share achieved the same night by *Baby Bob*, a challenging drama about a talking newborn. *American Fighter Pilot* soon joined the list of cancelled and forgotten reality shows. But with US troops taking up posts around the world, other channels were prepared to explore the potential of primetime militarism. On 27 May 2002, music network VH1 premiered *Military Diaries*, by R.J. Cutler, producer of *The War Room*, an Oscar-nominated documentary on the inner workings of the first Clinton presidential campaign. Much as Bruckheimer's movies give a uniformly sympathetic view of their military subjects, Cutler's *War Room*, though a skilful and entertaining film, was not a penetrating vision of the Clinton operation. Indeed, no 'friend of Bill' could have contrived a warmer impression of chief lieutenants James Carville and George Stephanopoulos than rendered by Cutler. Militainment producers, keen believers in the power of positive thinking, are about as incisive as the makers of soft drink commercials.

Cutler's show, in video diary fashion, was shot by the starring marines themselves, and included 'previously unseen combat footage' alongside GI's reflecting on their love of Mary J. Blige and Limp Bizkit. Like Bruckheimer, Cutler was not interested in analysing the war effort. Though he did not speak so blatantly of 'saluting the military', his show was intended to 'tell the story of what it's like to be a young man or woman in the armed forces right now'.[46] He too insisted that the Pentagon would have no editorial veto on the resulting footage, but as he set out to find 'people who are articulate, good at what they do, have a sense of humour and want to work with us to tell a story', they hardly needed one.

The Pentagon had for some time displayed an increasingly sophisticated understanding of entertainment media and how best to use them. Co-operation was not restricted to the producers of reality shows, with writers on *Judge Advocate General*, a fictional portrayal of naval tribunals, receiving briefings on panels established to try Al Q'aida and Taliban suspects before such information was provided to the regular press. The show was a major beneficiary of 11 September, leaping from twenty-eighth place in national ratings to tenth after the attacks, an improvement well noted by a jealous broadcasting industry.

For its own part, the US army now places short recruitment films on its website, featuring a surprisingly

---

46. PR Newswire, 4 April 2002.

glamorous array of cadets. One can only wonder how many viewers of a military-themed reality show might find their minds turning to enlistment, with the inevitable soft-focus portrayal of life in uniform appearing as a meaningful escape route from suburban inertia. Military existence, as packaged for primetime, is gruelling, yes, but noble and conferring dignity. There has always been a cynical aspect to military recruitment in its mass media applications, with commercials tailored to the bored and self-doubting ('could you be the best?', et cetera). On the part of governments obliged to maintain force levels, this could hardly be otherwise. Entertainment producers, however, have no mandate to assist them, and the United States government was quite specifically intended by the nation's founders to have no input into the products of an independent media. In 1993, Bill Nichols, referring to the *Cops* genre of reality TV, wrote that it 'aspires to non-friction',[47] reducing all possible subversion to a 'comestible glaze'. The glazed face of crime and punishment presented in the one-dimensional expanses of reality shows has been a consistent ratings hit throughout the period of America's love affair with 'zero tolerance', with its provisions for mandatory life sentences and ever more frequent recourse to the death penalty. Likewise, the military, as seen in these shows, are not the troops who have, by some accounts, killed more civilians in Afghanistan than Al Q'aida did in New York. 'Someone's

---

47. *Blurred Boundaries: Questions of Meaning in Contemporary Culture*, Indiana University Press, 1994.

idea of war', as Dan Rather put it, is a morally uncomplicated one: the forces of good doing battle with evil. The
Empire Striking Back.

This is not propaganda in the crude sense, not the novels
of 'beloved leader' Saddam Hussein, but such fare would
elicit little more than laughter from a Western audience.
Noam Chomsky once said that if one were to establish a
totalitarian state on an intelligent basis, the US system
would provide the perfect model. In much the same vein,
there is no better agent for the dissemination of a Bush-
approved image of the military than an independent,
Hollywood-trained production team, whose 'real footage'
from the front lines is filtered through fellow-traveller
hearts and minds. Bruckheimer, in his *Guardian* interview,
was willing to admit that 'both sides' – himself and the
Pentagon – had 'done very well out of it'. The storylines
reality TV grants prominence will not contextualise or
criticise the service personnel on display, let alone question
the policymakers who put them there. Just as *Cops*, with its
portrayal of crime as individual deviance, has neatly
encapsulated the ideology behind a corrections system that
holds three million Americans, *Profiles from the Front Line*
and the like are no more than high-production value
bunting, a flattering backdrop to the new imperialism. In
the Bogart era, Hollywood served a progressive, anti-fascist
propaganda function. Now it seems a broader call to arms is
the only message that its best and brightest understand.

At a time when US troops and 'military advisors' have
spread out across the globe, from Yemen to the Philippines,

Georgia to Colombia, their promotion back home as America's salt-of-the-earth, highly trained (though sensitive and music-loving) defenders is a gift to the war effort and its many beltway advocates. This is not a case of government dictating to the media, but a happy coincidence of interests that allows for the production of propaganda in a democratic guise. Silvio Berlusconi was at least obliged to purchase most of his media empire and win an election to secure the rest; Bush, Cheney and Rumsfeld have managed to do neither of these things, but, with the gracious assistance of Hollywood's well-meaning labour pool and the necklacing tendencies of a nation at war, are achieving much the same results.

R.J. Cutler, meanwhile, would seem to have acquired a taste for pushing the boundaries of reality TV – and, perhaps, for doing favours for the Bush administration. In September 2002, Rupert Murdoch's FX network announced its intention to produce, with Cutler in command, a political variation on the *American Idol* theme – auditioning not for a would-be popstar, but a 'people's' presidential candidate. Described by Cutler as *'The War Room* [see above] meets *American Idol'*, the show is based upon a similar Argentine format, *The People's Candidate*, which will pit sixteen hopefuls against each other, with a winner, selected by viewers, to contest the 2003 Congressional elections. The American version, seeking to galvanise an even more apathetic electorate (the highest turnout in a twentieth-century US presidential election being marginally over 60 per cent in 1960), aimed its sights straight at the White

House. This is anything but harmless fun, or, as Cutler claims (in apparent sincerity, and with more than a hint of the self-righteousness for which he has become well known), a democratic project 'making available to every American who is qualified, by virtue of the Constitution, the opportunity to run for President'.[48] The overwhelming likelihood is that the show, if successful, will be a yet better present for the democratically challenged Bush administration than free ad space for the military.

In 2000, over 90,000 votes were cast in Florida for the third-party candidacy of Ralph Nader (listed on the ballot as a Green, though not a member of the party), effectively killing the Kyoto agreement and more or less ensuring the appointment of pro-lifers to any Supreme Court vacancies that arise while Bush is at the helm, which brings with it a strong possibility that, by the close of the decade, American women will again be dying in back-alley abortions. (Nader, preferring not to discuss gynaecology, refused to confront this issue during the campaign. Of course, he will never have to.) With the two main parties running neck and neck at every level, a few thousand – indeed, a few hundred votes (or their exclusion from a recount at the hands of judges appointed by 'Bush the elected') – have proven to be all it takes to throw an election to the right. As Michael Moore points out, if a handful of minor hard-left candidates had not been on the ballot in Florida, Gore would have all but definitely taken the state, *even with Nader's megalomaniacal*

---

48. Drudge Report, 20 September 2002.

crusade in progress. A 'people's candidate', granted prominence by a national TV show and extensive funding from Rupert Murdoch, seems unlikely to take many votes from the GOP. The only third-party candidate to have done significant damage to a Republican president in recent memory, Ross Perot, did almost as much harm to the Clinton campaign, with a deranged brand of populism that appealed strongly to many who would have otherwise abstained. Perot, however, was in every sense an anomaly, and having emphasised the issue of deficit-reduction and his own status as a self-made billionaire obsessed with Vietnam vets missing in action, was bound to attract Conservative support. A 'people's candidate', without personal fortune, is far more likely to win the loyalty of those who would otherwise not vote – or cast their ballot for the hapless Democrats, unquestionably the worst entities in US politics, except for every other gun-toting, bible-bashing, tax-cuts-for-billionaires, or 'throw-your-vote-away' option.

The possibility is thus real that a candidate selected via a reality TV show could alter the outcome of the next presidential election. Splitting the vote under a simple plurality system has shown itself, throughout modern British, American and French political history to be the easiest path by far to Tory, Republican and Gaullist regimes. Murdoch's candidate, the eventual winner of the show, will not be obliged to contest the election, but it seems likely that s/he will do so, what with a priceless gift of free publicity and the spectacle of a 'People's Convention' to take place on the Mall in 2004 – on Independence Day, no less. Mr Cutler, once the hagiographer of Clinton's consiglieris, can only be assumed to have switched sides, and one wonders if his friendly status at the Pentagon might have led to further consultations with the powers that be on *American Candidate*. Rupert Murdoch, not known for actions harmful to Republican presidents, chose his producer well. It has been some forty years since television first decided a presidential election, in the legendary Nixon–Kennedy debates; if, in 2004, we should see the Republican and Democratic nominees debating alongside a third-party candidate given to the world by Messrs Murdoch and Cutler, elevating the game show to the level of a decisive electoral institution, the term 'reality TV', always dubious before, will have simply made itself redundant, 'reality' and 'television' turned interchangeable in an ultimate parody of democracy's aspirations to liberate humankind.

By the last scene of 1998 film *The Truman Show* the eponymous hero has realised that the community in which he has lived all his life is a vast TV construct, where the townspeople are actors who get into their starting position each morning before he wakes. It is a dome, sitting on the Hollywood hills, replete with its own weather, fake sun and moon, and Ed Harris' producer-God oversees and controls this world from a perch in the environment's fake sky. Truman, with the actor-townspeople chasing him, steals a boat and rows from the harbour, trying to gain freedom over the water. He survives a producer-created storm and then, in bright sunlight, gazing hopefully toward the horizon, hits a wall of sky. He has come up against the limit of his world; the populated pocket world screened to millions of viewers who delight in watching the contrived reality of his 'real life', has proven inescapable. And so the boat is pronged to the sky, the horizon's wall a blank delineation of the scope of his constructed reality. A terrific metaphor, and perhaps charged with familiarity for some who have spent time inside reality TV gameworlds. For us, it is not the case, or it is not all of the case, and our realities are not simply those dictated by television and mass media. Media have proliferated, yes, and Endemol would lead us into a world where the refractions of media representations of reality are present in the mirrors of every surface we encounter. In terms of how we react to such products, we may have grown more sophisticated, ironic and canny, but so far we are much as we were – sceptical, easily diverted, prone to investing too much of our time in media-spun trivialities. The latest trick – this plethora of cross-platform realia – is a clever one. Most of us were warned as children of the evils of TV, but we did not grow up in Truman's world, and need not, as adults, build ourselves a version of his prison.

INDEX